To Deana

MY WARMEST WISHES TO YOU FOR
THE MOST IMPORTANT THING IN
LIFE,YOUR GOOD HEALTH.

Jessica Richardson

The Ring and I

by Jessica Richardson

Library of Congress Catalog Number: 94- 92259

ISBN (Hard Cover) 0-9642398-1-7

Printed in the United States of America

Acknowledgements

Many thanks to all my family for supporting me in this endeavor.

Special thanks to my daughter, Heather Leveque, for all the help and caring that she gave so freely to both me and her father over the past fifteen years.

Thanks also to Heather's husband, Ernesto for all his thoughtfulness and understanding.

To my grandson, Alessandro Leveque, for his art work. He chose the trademark scroll and the beautiful handwriting that Philip was so well known for in his decorating for the jacket of this book as a tribute to his grandfather.

To my daughter, Cathy and her husband, Jeff McAlister who were always only a phone call away whenever I needed a shoulder to cry on and for helping with the editing and typing of the book.

I also wish to thank Mrs. Nina Trump and Mrs. Elsie Lunz, two very dear friends who have always inspired me with their way of life and for all of their support and prayers over the years.

To Dr. Gary Udd, Principal and Instructor at Castle Rock High School for his editorial advice.

My special thanks to Mr. Bill Stimson, Associate Professor of Journalism at Eastern Washington University. Mr. Stimson not only gave me the confidence to start writing my story, but he also gave me his expert guidance.

Thank you Cindy for pointing me in his direction.

Preface

It has been said that hind-sight is always better than foresight. I realized this many years ago, but much to my regret, it was too late to do anything about it. My father had passed away, and I never had the chance to thank him for saving me from a life of torment and ridicule. What better way to pay tribute to him than to begin this story on his birthday, February 15.

My father said to me one day, "Genty, you were cut out to be a genteel lady, but you are having a bit of bad luck." I don't know about the lady part, but I never thought of myself as being unlucky. There were times when unfortunate might have been a better choice of words.

My luckiest time of all was the day I met the love of my life, Philip Richardson. Then came the happiest time, the day we were married. My husband was exceptional. He was a skilled artist, a true craftsman and a perfectionist in every sense of the word. He was a man of compassion, yet he was also a very funny man. I was often asked if he was related to Bob Hope, but no. The only thing he had in common with the famous comedian was that he was an Englishman.

My story begins by describing some of the obstacles I was able to overcome as a child, the time I met this remarkable man and the trials and tribulations that we struggled through during our first years together.

Unfortunately, just when we thought we had reached a time of peace and tranquility, like a bolt from the blue, my husband became the victim of a very controversial scientific speculation. More to the point, he became victim of the catastrophe of the Swine Flu and Victoria Flu vaccines of 1976. In my opinion, he became just as much a hostage in his own body, for almost fifteen years, as those unfortunate men who were taken hostage in Lebanon.

We were robbed of what could have been some of the best years of our lives, instead, I watched him suffer the mental anquish of torment and frustration which accompanies brain damage. At that time, I was being intimidated, patronized and even stigmatized simply because I would not take "no" for an answer from doctors who said nothing could be done for Phil. I was determined not to give up so I frequently sought a second opinion, but with the exception of a small few, most doctors showed little interest. I think they preferred not to get involved in the search for answers to my husband's illness.

I was sometimes described as resembling a "tiger protecting her cub" and often referred to as a "persistent little shit." This only made me more determined to pursue what was now becoming a medical mystery.

As the years went by, I became very angry. I decided to write this book in order to handle my grief and to rid myself of all the bitterness and anger inside of me. I am also writing this, not only for my own peace of mind, but for the benefit of other unsuspecting victims.

I want everyone to know, not just my circle of friends, but the whole world. I want others to know just exactly how I feel, which is to say, "In my opinion, what happened to my husband, as a result of the Swine Flu and Victoria Flu vaccines should never have happened."

The following account is dedicated, IN LOVING MEMORY, to my father--Joseph Clay and my husband--Philip Richardson.

The Clay Family

I was born on January 22, 1915, the youngest of three girls. My brother came along seven years later. The small council house that my parents rented, which was to become their home for the next forty years, was in a fair-sized town called Doncaster in Yorkshire, England. The town was noted for its sport of kings and its famous horse race, the *Doncaster St. Leger,* which usually attracted one or more of the Royal Family. This race was the highlight of a full week of racing which took place the first week in September when most of the working class took their week's vacation. The majority of these people rested their hopes all-year-round on picking the winning horses and accumulating a small fortune.

My father, or *Little Joe* as he was affectionately called, was small in stature but giant in principles. He was very fond of horses. His one ambition in life was to be a jockey and part of the racing fraternity. During St. Leger week, he was always on the course at the crack of dawn to see the thoroughbreds exercising in hopes of spotting a winner, like the early bird catching the worm. He always said there was only one way to follow a horse successfully and that was with a pail and shovel. He also often stated, "The certainty of racing is the uncertainty of it."

The main work at that time was coal mining. There were many collieries within a few miles of each other and Little Joe was sent down the mine at an early age, much to his chagrin. He eventually got out, and in time, served his apprenticeship as an iron molder.

When the call of duty came to serve his country in 1914, he volunteered to join the army. We were at war with

Germany! He took leave of my mother a few months before I was born.

Six months after I was born, I became ill with bronchitis, which left me very weak. I developed a severe case of rickets, a disease of infancy for which the only treatment was plenty of fresh air and sunlight. This caused my legs to become very badly deformed. Father was never told of my deformity.

By this time I was two years old, and with Father away in the service, it was Mother's tender-loving care that enabled me to regain some of my strength. Unfortunately, I was not able to walk. I couldn't even stand on my own two feet. My legs looked like two bent hooks.

I was taken to an infirmary but because of the great demand on hospitals, doctors and nurses, there was little help available for anything that was not war related. I was lucky to be supplied with a wooden splint and foot rest for each leg as an alternative to braces. Each leg was bound to the splint with wads of cotton and bandages. From what I was told, this could not have been too unpleasant as I was in no physical pain. I was taken for daily outings in a pram (perambulator) in the hopes of being able to catch a little sunshine, and once a week checked into the infirmary for a change of bandages.

I spent nearly six years of life in a sitting position. I can see where this might have stunted my growth. I only made it to 4' 9", but I must admit, this often worked to my advantage. I often got special attention and care because I was so small.

My sisters, Lucie the oldest, and Elsie, were already in school. The compulsory starting age was five. In the meantime, I was enrolled in the Guild School for children of all ages. Mother told me she enjoyed this period because we were involved in fund raising for the school. Alexandra Rose Day was a special day at the Guild School when all the prams were decorated from top to bottom with roses and paraded through the downtown streets. We all carried baskets of artificial roses which were sold, with all the proceeds going to the school.

Just before the war ended, Father was given an honorable discharge because of wounds received while serving in the Balkans. However, before returning home he was sent directly to a hospital in the city of Leeds to recuperate. While there, like many others, he was given the opportunity to attend the Leeds School of Art as a part of a rehabilitation program. He found interest in wood carving and brought home several attractive jewelry boxes that he had carved, but realized to do this for a living would be too time consuming and more just a labor of love.

Since he was no longer capable of working at his trade, he needed to earn enough money to subsidize his meager disabilitypension. He also made it perfectly clear that he would not apply for any public assistance. He would simply find lighter work. Even this was difficult at times because he also was stricken with malaria during the war. This caused him severe headaches about once a month and during those episodes he was unable to work at anything.

I don't remember the first meeting with my father, but apparently, he was shocked at my disability and immediately was determined to do something about it. I learned much later that, as a young man, he and his good friend Billy Fox (the local undertaker) had teamed up to train their respective brothers in sprinting. They were part of a running team known as the Doncaster Harriers. He assured Mother he knew a lot about legs, and if he could help his brother to run, he could at least help his little daughter to walk.

The next few years were hard for me to understand. I came to dislike this strange man who suddenly had taken charge of our home. I could only think he came to hurt me. First he rubbed by legs with oil and then he massaged them. After that he put hot and cold packs on my aching legs. One day he came home with a pair of leather boots which came up to my knees. Mother disapproved of this approach which caused one of many arguments. However, once he got my legs into the boots, she knew he was on the right track.

Lacing these boots was a difficult matter. It was so painful for me, I cried at every attempt. At this point I was too young to understand that this was serious and that I might never walk, but I was not too young to remember the terrible pain. Day after day, and for what seemed like an eternity, those boots finally came together and were laced all the way to the top, which was a victory in itself.

Now came the hard part of letting go of the pram and trying to stand. From here on, Mother took over. As she would with a year-old baby, she was able to help me to take those first few steps. She continued to work diligently with me until at the age of six I was able to walk.

After I learned to walk, Father proceeded to get work. He began by purchasing a small horse and cart, a ladder, some garden tools and a set of chimney sweep brushes. He then had some cards printed which read, "***Little Joe Clay, Handyman, No Job Too Small.***" His efforts paid off quite nicely, enough to provide for us.

My brother, Walter, was born a year after my father started his own business. Father was happy to have a son and had him baptized in the Catholic Church as part of a promise he had made. After he had been wounded in the war, he was taken care of by nuns. Before he was sent home, he asked what he could do to repay them for their kindness. They requested simply that his children be sent to a Catholic school and, if any others came along, to have them baptized in the Catholic Church. Being a man of his word, he did just that. To complete the promise, Lucie and Elsie were transferred to St. Peter's School.

When I started walking comfortably, I was taken from the Guild school to join them at St. Peter's School. The school was more than a mile away so I rode there on the tram for one penny. After getting off of the tram downtown, I still had three or four blocks to walk. Of course, my mother took me the first day which was truly a blessing.

As we stepped off of the tram that first day and proceeded toward High Street, I stopped to look in a large store window. For the first time, I saw myself in the glass, as others could see me. I was horrified. How could something like this happen to me? I pleaded to go home, but my mother wasn't about to give in. It was different at the Guild school. Everyone was crippled. But, what would these school kids think of me and my ugly legs?

Most of the teachers at St. Peter's were nuns so I was left in the capable hands of Sister Mary Patricia. She did her best to convince me that everything would be all right when my mother was gone.

Lucie and Elsie now had the responsibility of watching over me during lunchtime and making sure that I got the tram home. Looking back on those years, I often wondered if they resented all the attention focused on me. If they did, they certainly didn't show it.

Having to start in the first standard (first grade), although I was two years older, didn't matter to me because I was no bigger than the rest of the class. I soon found out, however, that five-year-olds can be very mean. I was called all kinds of names which, had I been normal, would have been funny. But, I was a newcomer and my legs were deformed. I just hated them for calling me names. I kept to myself most days and tried to make up for lost time. This new school was a challenge for me.

We girls went to Mass at the Catholic Church on Sunday. On occasions Father would go with us. We sat with the children. Father would sit at the back of the church and read a book about horse racing or study racing forms while he waited for us, but he never failed to put money in the collection plate.

After going home for breakfast, he would take us for a walk in the beautiful woods of Sandle Beat. This was a peaceful, picturesque setting with the sweet smell of honeysuckle everywhere. This was one of our favourite spots.

We often went there for picnics in the summer when all the colorful wild-flowers were in bloom. In the spring, what appeared like a sea of blue was actually an abundance of the lovely blue bells blowing in the March winds. Whenever I hear the song, "Mary My Scotch Blue Bell," I remember this place with a certain amount of nostalgia. I'm afraid sister Elsie didn't share these memories of the woods. She was so fearful of frogs. We all knew the minute she had spotted one of them because she would let out a shriek that could surely raise the dead.

While on our Sunday adventure at Sandle Beat, we would be sure to watch the time carefully. At Mother's insistence, we had to be home by 1:00 p.m. sharp for Sunday dinner.

Sunday dinner was always a special treat. There was a roast of some kind, mashed potatoes and gravy, and the traditional Yorkshire pudding. This was usually topped off with Mother's home-made pie or pudding for a sweet (dessert).

Tea time at 5 p.m. was just as special because of her delicious bread. She made these large, round flat-bread cakes. Mother would slice and butter them (my mouth waters at the thought). We ate these with good Cheshire cheese and celery. Mother also used her method of "*killing two birds with one stone*" by serving us either stewed prunes or stewed rhubarb with custard. I preferred this method to the alternative of the weekly dose of tea made from Senna pods or castor oil--"Yuk."

Before going any further, I think I should write about the real Mr. and Mrs. Joseph Clay. I'm sure that at sometime or another we have all voiced our opinion about certain couples. For example, "Whatever made her marry him or him marry her." Without meaning any disrespect, I often wondered this about my parents. They were worlds apart yet so much alike in many ways, especially in their principles. It pains me to say this, but I never saw them embrace although they must have loved at sometime; they had four children. Maybe, like many people those days, it was hard to show their affection for each other.

My mother, Mary Elizabeth (Libby), was a slightly built lady with an 18 inch waist. She had an attractive face with high cheek bones and her blue-grey eyes were set wide apart. As long as I can remember, she always appeared older than her years. Maybe it was because she dressed very modestly. In addition, cleanliness was definitely next to Godliness for her.

Mother's maiden name was Orton and her family consisted of six sisters and six brothers. Like most of her sisters, she worked in domestic service before she married. This was good experience for her as she was a perfect housekeeper. However, I hasten to say that although she was so proud of the way she kept our home, she soon became a slave to it.

There were no modern appliances which we take so much for granted these days, no electricity and no hot water (perish the thought). At least the water was running and we didn't have to go outside for it. We had no bathroom, but we did have an outdoor toilet with running water. The toilet was housed in a brick building attached to a coal house situated about twenty feet from the back of our house.

Much to Mother's dismay, it seemed that no sooner had she scrubbed out the toilet and cleaned off the steps that coal would be delivered, covering everything with coal dust. This was one of her many pet peeves. Others included Father using the wrong towel, usually the baby's white one--heaven forbid, and not cleaning his boots on the door mat before entering the house. The sparks really lit up on such occasions.

They had many fights but only verbal, never physical. Mother would shed a few tears. Father often told us it was all right for us to take her part (side) and that he would understand if we did. His point of view was that she did too much complaining over trivial things. On the other hand, if the paper boy was late with Father's morning paper that was a real catastrophe for him.

I remember many pleasant evenings when we played a game called <u>Put and Take</u> or <u>Dominoes</u>. We were shown how to play <u>Whist</u> so that, as we grew older, we could go to a <u>Whist</u>

drive at some local church hall or other place of entertainment. _Whist_ is a card game with two couples at each table and sometimes as many as twenty-five tables. A total of twenty-four games were played with a break at halftime for refreshments. Prizes were awarded for the highest scores and sometimes a dance would follow.

Because Father only had the bare essentials of schooling, he concentrated on educating himself by reading. We had two daily newspapers and three on Sundays which he read from front to back. He also had many books about history which was his favourite subject. At times he would entertain us by reciting works of William Shakespeare or quotes from famous statesmen like Disraeli, Gladstone and Lloyd George. Little Joe had a thirst for knowledge of American history, especially famous presidents such as George Washington and Abraham Lincoln. He had memorized the Declaration of Independence.

I couldn't speak for my sisters but I wasn't aware that any of these people had even existed. I thought Father was making it all up. However, I know now, all this was not merely a figment of his imagination but a part of the great annals of history. I can say in all sincerity that, yes, Little Joe Clay was truly a remarkable and diverse man.

Mother was also remarkable in the way she managed to do everything herself. She took care of us, cleaned house and did the wash which included ironing and starching. Wash day was a full, hard-day's work in itself. The only thing she expected of us was washing dishes and running errands to the grocery store.

Like most housewives, she took in lodgers for bed and breakfast during race week when the town was filled with racegoers from near and far. We were lucky enough to get two gentlemen to stay with us. Mr. Schumm was from Middlesbrough and owned a butcher business and the other was Mr. Sherwood who was in the fish-and-chip business. These two must have thought they had found a home away from home because they came every year for fifteen years. This was

Mother's way of providing a few little extras for us. When the week was over we were taken downtown to buy new clothes and a supply of wool for her knitting.

We were usually treated to the fair which ended the week of activities during the *Doncaster St. Leger.* More often than not, this would be her only trip to town during the year. I remember that it was a happy occasion and gave her a sense of accomplishment. Except for a walk in the park on summer evenings, Mother rarely went far away.

Mother was content to stay home with her knitting which was another one of her accomplishments. We never wore a store-bought sweater, she always made them. I never saw her sit down without knitting needles and she taught it to all of us at an early age. I can see her now in her rocking chair knitting away as though she had resigned herself to this for the rest of her life, yet she was still so young. Maybe she was just very tired, and this was a source of relaxation for her.

Before we were all sent to the Catholic Church, Mother used to take us to the nearby Gospel Hall. I know she enjoyed the hymn singing. On rare occasions, throughout years, she would surprise us with a rendition of her favourite hymn, "Abide With Me." I do so wish I could have known what she was like as a young girl.

Getting back to my school years, it seemed like I never would be accepted by the girls. The boys weren't so bad. At least they would talk to me when I sat next to them in class. I developed a crush on a boy whose last name was Masarella. He was so good looking, as was his entire family. The name, Masarella, did not indicate to me that he was Italian. As far as I knew there were only two kinds of people, Protestants and Catholics, and this had nothing to do with their names. The Masarella boy came from a large family that was in the ice cream business. Believe me, it didn't take long to find out that the Italians made the best ice cream.

By the time I reached age 10, I was sent for an evaluation to determine if I was eligible to receive therapy at a new school that employed an open-air concept. Besides the rickets, I was found to have flat feet, weak ankles, my spine was affected, and one shoulder was higher than the other. I spent one full year at this health-oriented facility. We got a certain amount of schooling but the emphasis was on therapeutic exercises. There was a one-hour nap outside in the fresh air every day after lunch. This was all free, as well as the transportation and a cup of hot chocolate upon arrival. I will forever remember the aroma of that delicious treat. I went back to St. Peters a much stronger person and ready to do more catching up. By this time Lucie had already left school and, at age fourteen, went to work as a domestic servant.

Father bought a piece of land, about half an acre, in a rural area called Bessacarr. This land was approximately four miles from our home and was surrounded by three or four estates owned by upper-class people. One estate was owned by Mr. Hutchinson who was in the building and construction business. He and Father became good friends and remained so for the rest of their lives. Father was able to render services to these estates. Mr. Hutchinson hired him to clear away the debris from construction sites. On these occasions Father was usually able to pick up a few discarded items which would serve some purpose for his newly acquired land.

Father eventually built himself a hut which was just big enough to hold a couch for himself to lie down and also a wood stove to boil water for his life-saving cup of tea. Best of all, he could now provide a stable for his horse. In time he grew a small vegetable garden, a flower garden and raised a few chickens and ducks. It took a while for him to get all those things in working order so he was often gone from sun up to sun down.

We couldn't help but notice if he were late, as Mother would get very worried and start pacing the street until she spotted him turning the corner on his trusty bicycle. This told us she really did care for him but was too stubborn to admit it.

He was much the same way but we always knew for sure that he showed her a great deal of respect.

Those days a telephone was simply unheard of among the working class, so they agreed that if Father had something important on his agenda and couldn't make it home before dark that he would stay overnight at his new establishment. He would consider it important if a batch of baby chicks or ducklings were due to be hatched. He would stay to protect them from small wild-life intruders during the night.

On occasions there were a few weaklings born, and he would promptly bring them home for some of Mother's care. I think being needed by something so small was really her cup of tea. It was a delight to watch her hovering like a mother hen over these fuzzy, little, feathered creatures. They were put in a basket and placed in front of the fire, under her watchful eye, until they were strong enough to go back to their families.

I remember one time she got so attached to a duckling that she decided to keep it for while. It followed her everywhere and looked so quaint strutting along behind her with its neck stretching into the air. One day when Mother went to the door to pick up the mail, the door slammed behind her before the little creature made it through. It got trapped and died instantly. She was devastated and couldn't bring herself to keep another one as a pet.

Our family was growing up and so was the neighborhood. Little Walter was not so little anymore. He was really no trouble at all and he had a happy disposition. He soon made friends with the little kids on our street. We had a new family move into the neighborhood, the Taylors who had five children. One of the children whose name was Clara was my age and we soon became good friends.

Their youngest was a boy named Claude. He was about Walter's age and, together with two other boys, Kenneth Turner and Ernie Andrews, they became inseparable. As they grew older, they had such great times. I don't ever recall them being cruel or destructive, only the natural dare-devil kind of things that come from being boys. They were all crazy about soccer and played it at every opportunity. There was no doubt that Mother was very fond of these boys.

Walter was exceptionally good at soccer and played all through school. He also turned out to be very handsome, although I never let him think so, and he had a wonderful smile because of his good teeth. I was always pestering him to make sure he cleaned his teeth regularly and he often reminded me about that in later years.

I can see him now kidding around with Mother and pouncing on her in what he called a rugby tackle. Then he would pick her up and twirl her around. She was so thin and frail and would profess to be angry but we knew she thrived on the attention. It was food for her soul.

One thing stands out in my memory of this time in our lives. So many people were dying from tuberculosis, a lot of them were children. I felt so sad when, right next door to us, a family lost a three year old boy and a fifteen year old girl. Many children were sent to sanitariums for treatment but very often this was too late.

The Racing Business

Elsie and Lucie had their own jobs, but throughout the racing season they worked two jobs. When Elsie left school at fourteen, she got a job in domestic service as a cook. She turned out to be a very good one. She excelled in baking, and like Mother, she was a real soft touch. One only had to pay her the smallest compliment, and she would shower him with her tantalizing treats.

By now Lucie was tired of working as a maid and found a job as an usherette at the Arcadia Theater in the evenings. This came just as Dad was about to announce his plans to take a new direction. Lucie would be free during the day and could fit into his plan very nicely.

It seems Mr. Hutchinson had contracted to build a new housing project not far from the race course. These were going to be good, quality homes in the price range to suit the upper class. This provided more work that was closer to home for Father. Sometimes Father was a watchman for the building sites on weekends and this is where his new idea took shape. He figured that most working men could afford to gamble occasionally, especially in a racing town like Doncaster where betting on horses was almost a way of life. So, he decided to go into the business of being a bookie and taking bets just on the horses. This was not the type of bookie you see on the course but in a home office which would have to be licensed to make it legal.

None of us could see the sense in such a move. It's not like he had a notion that he could make a lot of money, he was too smart for that. I think it was his long-time desire of wanting to be a jockey which had already passed him by. Now, he could at least be part of the excitement that draws people into the racing circle.

Despite Mother's protests, Father went on with his new-found interest. We were never forced into helping him, but because of his powers of gentle persuasion, we went along with him. To do otherwise would have been like flogging a dead horse.

I'm sure he had studied this venture thoroughly and his first move was to turn our home into a little shop. Of course, he ran into a few obstacles before obtaining a license from the city council to sell a few staples like bundles of wood for kindling, candles, matches, cigarettes, and candy. This was just a sprat to catch a mackerel.

We had an oversized shed in the backyard which he made into an office so that the clients could sit and study the racing forms. There was, however, a big snag. Even though betting was legal at the time, it could only be done on a credit basis. In other words, one must have an account and settle up at the month-end either by a statement of losses or a check in the amount of winnings. It went without saying, this was taking a big enough risk when done on a large scale among the upper class where a gentleman's word was his bond. On a much smaller scale, among the working class, the risk was much greater. Father was aware of the great risks involved, but he hadn't given a second thought to the fact that we were all completely incompetent when it came to clerical work. It would also be very difficult without a telephone.

Father did the same as many others in the same situation. He broke the law by taking cash only and ran the risk of being caught. The worst that could happen was to lose his license so he never felt too guilty in breaking the law. The rest of us felt a little scared especially since the police had a sentry box at the top of the street. Father tried to assure us that the police themselves were known to make bets and not just on horses.

"Look," said Father. "The Bobbies bet on the horses and won't bother a small businessman like me. They most likely will look the other way or concentrate on more serious matters, like the houses of ill-repute on their beat."

Mother would make tea for the workers on the construction sites, and Father would deliver it. At the same time, he would pick up their betting slips and bring them back to the office. Lucie stayed at home to help Mother with the shop and take the bets from every other Tom, Dick or Harry. This was very hard on Mother. She normally took everything in stride, but this was above and beyond her duty as a housewife. Her home was not her own anymore as it was being invaded by strangers who were trying to beat the racing system at all odds. I was only too glad to be in school, at least for the time being.

There was also another side of this gambling scene which attracted all kinds of waifs and strays in the form of teenage, apprentice jockeys. This was much to the delight of many young ladies, including my sisters. These young men were mostly from out of town and would stay at the home of the horse owners and trainers. Somehow, many of them found their way to our door step. The word always got around that Mother was a soft touch for a free meal.

Father was still able to maintain his parcel of land. Being an early riser, he would ride his bicycle to Bessacarr, tend to his horse and poultry, and be back in time for his regular routine. I remember he always brought fresh eggs, too, so we added those to our shop supplies.

He kept going all right, but things didn't always run smoothly. I'm sure there were times when he thought he had bitten off more than he could chew. This became evident when the big races came along, like the Ascot Gold Cup, the Epsom Derby, and the Doncaster St. Leger. These races attracted more than the average amount of punters (betters).

Father would be obliged to hedge off money from two or three horses in order to balance his books otherwise he could be caught napping and take a big loss. Lucie would have to take the money and place it on the horses in question with some other (cash) office like ours. She would be what was called a *bookies runner,* except she rode her bicycle. Many times she barely had time to get there before the start of the race. On these occasions, and because these other offices had a telephone, Lucie would wait for the results of the race and then hurry to tell Father the good or bad news. The rest of the day's results would appear in the evening paper so Lucie would help by going through all the bets and figure out the winnings and losses before she went to her evening job at the theater. When Elsie had her day off, she was able to give Lucie a break and work in her place.

This routine went on continuously. Father was determined to see it through even after taking quite a beating, and I must say this in his favour, he was the soul of honesty and a good sport. He always paid up with a smile.

There were times when he was temporarily, financially embarrassed, as he so eloquently put it. He would find it necessary to borrow money which usually meant a trip to the pawn shop. He owned a number of valuable gold coins and a solid-gold watch but on occasion would put up his land for collateral.

The end of the flat racing season was marked by a big race called the Manchester November Handicap after which we all gave a sigh of relief. We could then relax and enjoy our spare time until next March.

Father spent more time at Bessacarr but as the bleak, cold and foggy days came along he took advantage of the break and caught up with his reading. He also did a bit of writing in the style of Olde English.

Christmas

I was so happy that Christmas was never interrupted by the horse racing. This was my favourite time of year, not so much for the gifts I received, but for the peace and tranquility in our home. Mother and Father were on better terms and the atmosphere was filled with a sense of warmth and understanding. Those Christmas days were observed with a joyous celebrating of the birth of Jesus Christ, much more than in today's troubled world. It seemed as though there was a greater spiritual feeling among the communities, and I wanted all those wonderful feelings to stay in my heart forever.

We always had a lovely Christmas tree which was put up and decorated about ten days before Christmas and taken down January 6th on the feast of Epiphany. We had those quaint little ornaments of yesteryear. I remember, most of all, the bright colored birds with tails like silk, pink sugar pigs, mice that hung by their tails, chocolate soldiers and Santa's, garlands and lanterns hanging from the ceiling. Of course, there was the traditional holly and mistletoe.

Mother did her baking, as usual. The fruit cakes and Christmas puddings were made well in advance. Then came the cookies; individual mince, lemon curd and jam tarts and her special scones. Before the Christmas pudding was served with white sauce, Mother would insert lucky silver charms and coins. If one were to find one of these charms it was considered very good luck.

I never tasted turkey until I came to America. Our Christmas dinner was either a cockerel, which was young and tender, or a couple of wild rabbits. I must not forget the assortment of home made wines like elderberry, rhubarb, dandelion and parsnip. Every tradesman that came to the house was invited in for a glass of wine and a choice of Mother's tarts.

Apart from the carnival and fair during race week, we spent very little on entertainment, but we were allowed to go to the pantomimes which appeared at the Grand Theatre every Christmas. This was part of the Christmas festivities for people of all ages. I couldn't wait to see the likes of Cinderella, Little Red Riding Hood and all the fairy tale characters. The rest of the year the Grand Theater was reserved for musicals or variety shows. We were also able to go to the Arcadia which was strictly for plays. Lucie was allowed one free pass every week, which she usually gave to Father. He really preferred the movies and was a big fan of the great actors like the Barrymores, Greta Garbo, and Sir Lawrence Olivier. He didn't care much for comedy films. I smile when I think of him sitting in the front row. As I have said, he was a small man so he could see better up front. It suited his pocket better because those seats only cost four pence. He had no time for those who paid much more to see the same show in order to "put on the dog," or "show off" by sitting in the higher priced seats.

Boxing Day was a national holiday in England and celebrated the day after Christmas. I'm sure most people have heard different versions of Boxing Day. As I recall, in Yorkshire if one worked in service for the nobility, it was expected that all the staff would be on duty for Christmas day. The next day the situation would be reversed as the nobility would serve dinner (a full course Christmas meal) to their servants. One was not given a Christmas present, the term was Christmas Box. At this dinner they received their Christmas Box, usually in the form of a cash bonus, in appreciation for good services, hence the term--Boxing Day. There was also another tradition on this day when the gentry would send out Christmas Boxes to the poor, elderly people living in the alms houses. This would be in the form of a box of wholesome food, a voucher for a supply of coal, or both.

There were those who preferred to observe Christmas day strictly as a holy day and do their merry making on Boxing Day. I must mention that Christmas would not be complete for me without the singing of carols and Christmas hymns. To this day I love to sing and especially as part of the Christmas tradition.

Growing Up

After the holiday season was over, and we were well into the wintery days of January and the scattering of snow, it wasn't always easy to keep warm without central heating. However, we seemed to get through it with plenty of warm clothing and the welcoming sight and feel of the roaring fire when we got home from school. My knees were always the coldest part of me.

On weekends, when things seemed a little dull, Father would get on his soap box and attempt to relieve the monotony. We would listen to his rendition of the man who stood in the market place for forty years selling pills or the tipster selling his tips on the race course. Usually, the finale was Brutus (the Roman General) and his famous speech: "Friends, Romans, Countrymen, lend me your ears. I come to bury Caesar not to praise him." This was always followed by a definition of those historical words.

He could also be really funny when the occasion arose, like teasing us for being afraid of the dark. This was because we took a lighted candle with us when we went to the toilet at night.

He was able to make his point one day, as he was reading the news headlines to us, "Amy Johnson Flies Solo Across the Ocean at Night." Then he turned to us and said, "Just imagine that brave young woman, flying all alone in the dark over shark-infested waters and my daughters can't even go to shit without a candle." I thought that was so funny and laugh every time I think of it, even though it was a crushing blow to our egos.

Before my turn came to be a bookie's runner, one of my fondest dreams came true. I got my first pair of shoes. This was more by good luck than management. Mr. Hutchinson, who had two daughters of his own, would often give away the girls' cast-off clothing. Although we were never poor, Father would stand by his motto of "never ask and never refuse." So, he graciously accepted their offerings. Lucie and Elsie were always happy for anything extra in clothing but being such a shrimp, I was never on the receiving end of such quality items.

Father had brought home a package and while we were going through the contents we came across a pair of brown shoes. I looked on while my sisters both tried on the shoes, but they were much too small. I felt like Cinderella waiting to try on the famous glass slipper.

"What's the use," I said. "I wouldn't be allowed to wear them, even if they did fit."

It had been made so clear to me that I could not wear low shoes because they did not provide the support for my weak legs and ankles. However, those brown shoes did fit me, and when my mother saw the look of joy on my face, she didn't have the heart to take them away from me. We compromised in that Mother said I could keep them but only wear them occasionally and hang on to my black boots. I was so delighted that I literally felt I was in seventh heaven.

After this victory, there was no stopping me. Learning to ride a bicycle became a must. I wasn't about to become a "runner" on foot when the others were provided with a bicycle. So, with a lot of help, it didn't take me long to master bike riding.

Mr. Hutchinson's project was completed and he retired from business. Father always kept in touch with him, especially when Mr. Hutchinson's health started failing. Father was a big help to his family. We encountered another builder, named Firth, whose contracts were mostly commercial sites. Many of our previous clientele found work with this firm and so the bookie business continued. Father would just follow them around with the same ruse of Mother's good tea making, which was often called "Sergeant Major's Tea." I'm sure that was meant as a compliment.

Just before I left elementary school, Father tried to talk me into going on to high school. This was not free but it was not compulsory, either. So, I did the same as my sisters--I turned him down, but for different reasons. Knowing from his own experiences how important education was, he was willing to pay for all of us. This was a chance he never had but he could not convince us. He must have been very disappointed.

Lucie and Elsie didn't particularly like school so they were glad to start working to make their own money as soon as possible. I like to think I had a legitimate excuse. First of all, I had missed three years of elementary school and even though I was able to catch up somewhat, I still didn't have enough confidence. The real reason was more personal. I had already suffered enough torment and ridicule from the young students at St. Peter's. I didn't think I could face more of the same embarrassment from high school teenagers as they could even be worse. I often felt sorry that I didn't accept Father's offer, especially when he said he knew I could do it. I did so want to please him because he believed in me. I can still hear him saying, "Never let it be said your mother bred a jibber."

My last year at St. Peter's was by far the most pleasant because I got very good marks. Considering the circumstances, and although I say so myself, the reports of my personal behavior were always very favourable. However, the best part was my friendship with three girls. After being away for a number of years, Nora Turley and Aurelia Scully were returnees. The third one, Rose Fiori, was a newcomer. She was a pretty girl with very dark, brown eyes and beautiful, dark, wavy hair. Her face stands out so vividly in my mind. From my knowledge today, I would say Rose either had sinus problems or allergies. At times she seemed so stressful from constantly drying her eyes and her nose would be sore from sneezing and nasal drip. Regardless, I took a liking to her right away. My life was so much happier because of those three friends, even though it was for such a short time. I don't remember seeing them again after my school years but whenever I think about them it gives me a warm feeling inside.

By this time Lucie had met and married a young man who worked with her at the Arcadia Theatre. She continued to help us for a while with the betting business until I got used to it. I started out by delivering the tea to the workmen and bringing their bets back to the office. I carried out the instructions to keep the cash separate from the slips of paper on which the bets were written. I was a little scared at first and wondered what I would say if I were ever approached by a police officer. I remembered that Father had said they wouldn't bother us, we were small potatoes. In my case, I could add, small fry.

I soon learned all the aspects of this "business" and made a little pocket money too. If the workers had a winning day, I was given tips. When I collected Mother's tea money there was usually a little extra for me, which made it worthwhile. I was also quick at figures which was an advantage in being able to total a client's winnings, on place betting, and on doubles or trebles.

I got so involved that, I have to admit, there were times when I could easily have become a compulsive gambler at a very young age. I often wondered if it ever affected Father that way, but I know his character was such that he would never submit to that kind of weakness. He did like to bet, but only to a point. His interest was more in the horses themselves and the breeding of the noble beast, rather that how fast they could run.

Anyway, the first big race that came along for me to do the running was the Derby (pronounced "Darby" in England). This was a race for three-year-olds and was held at Epsom Downs in Surrey every year, much in the same way as the Kentucky Derby is run in this country but without as much pomp and circumstance. I wish I could remember the name of the winner that year, but I only remember that I was nervous because the offices where I took Father's hedging money were a much bigger outfit and were often subject to being raided by the police for taking ready cash. It didn't seem to deter them. It was more or less a routine thing and they usually ended up just paying a fine.

I was getting much more adept at riding a bicycle, having to make two or three runs some days. Just like my sisters had done before me, I would wait for the results of the race and come flying home with the news. Riding that bike was a blessing in disguise to me, but I wasn't aware it was happening. The more I rode, the more I was exercising my legs and the more exercise, the more strength I gained, very slowly but surely. This was the best therapy possible and I did it for almost three years. I'm ashamed to admit that before I was through with the job I did an awful lot of complaining.

Lucie had her first baby, a little girl named Jean. So, she was out of commission for a while. This meant that Elsie and I had more to do during this short spell. Lucie's husband, Eric Fitzgeorge, had acquired a job at the Danum Bakery which made them a little better off financially. She still came to help us out on occasions and would bring the baby for Mother to dote on. Needless to say, this always brightened Mother's day. She was in all her glory, fussing over her first grandchild and putting her knitting skills to work on all the baby clothes.

Although I wasn't allowed to do outside work because I was considered on the delicate side, I did welcome a change in helping Lucie and Eric by taking care of Jean. This was good experience for me because later on I did this for a number of our neighbors and felt a little bit more independent.

I was also able to go with Elsie to some of the *Whist* drives on Friday nights. It was difficult for us to get partners at first because some of the so-called "avid card players" didn't want to take a chance on such young people. However, because of Father's teaching, our knowledge of the game soon surprised them all, and we often came away with prizes. I would have liked to have done more with Elsie. She was so outgoing and friendly with everyone, but she also liked to date and she did have some very nice boy friends. I realized from the start that three was considered a crowd.

Before this particular racing season ended, Father took me to the Doncaster meet one day while the rest of the family held down the fort. I had often been with Elsie to see the horses exercise in the early morning but mostly in hopes of catching a glimpse of some of the famous jockeys, such as Gordon Richards who was eventually knighted by the Queen. There was also Freddy Fox, Lester Piggott and many others. Some days we had quite a wait because of the thick, grey fog, but I had never actually seen a real race with the jockeys in their coloured silks. Father took time on this day to point out the many aspects of horse racing, not just the race itself which was over in a matter of minutes.

There were so many operations, including the sales of horses at various ages. This was usually seen prior to the start of a meet. There were vendors who were allowed only on the outside and at the entrance of the course. I can hear them now shouting, "Get your famous Nutthalls Mintoes and Parkinson's Royal Doncaster Butterscotch." If the Royal Family did indeed purchase any product, then the manufacturer was allowed to add Royal to their advertising. Incidently, that butterscotch was a delicious candy.

Among the many tipsters on the free course, I saw a very tall, black man. I was told that he came from Africa and he was dressed in native garb. He called himself Prince Monalulu. He was very colorful as was his language, which left a bad taste in my mouth. He always attracted a large crowd with his famous, "I've got a horse to beat the favourite."

I was mostly fascinated by the Tic-Tac system. A special segment of the grandstands was reserved for those professionally trained men in the art of Tic-Tac. They were paid a fee by a number of bookies who put up their stands in various parts of the free course, but within a certain radius. From their position in the grandstands, the Tic-Tacs were able, with the help of binoculars, to observe and obtain all kinds of valuable information. Of special importance was the condition of the horses as they were paraded around the paddock prior to the start of the race. These Tic-Tacs would then pass this information on to the bookies by wearing white gloves and using signal codes. This was done in much the same way as a baseball coach signals his players. For the bookies, it was a way of letting them know which horses were being bet on heavily and when it was time to do any hedging in order to balance their book.

I was very impressed by this procedure but disillusioned when Father told me the Tic-Tacs obtained inside information as to whether a horse was really trying all out to win or just in the race for a trial run, in which case they used designated jockeys. I thought that was downright cheating, like an athlete throwing a game. I guess the owners thought nothing of it and considered it good business to wait for another race when the odds on their horse were more lucrative. I'm sure this is what Father had in mind when he said, "The certainty of racing is the uncertainty of it."

As the winter came upon us once again, I spent quite a bit of time with my friend, Clara Taylor. She had turned into quite a character. She had straight, black hair with a fringe (bangs) and reminded me so much of Clara Bow, the silent screen actress. Betty Burns, another local girlfriend of ours, was very intelligent. She was also quite attractive, with beautiful red, curly hair. As I recall, she went to high school and was only home on weekends, so our time with her was short and sweet. She went on to nursing school. Betty, in later years, was in some branch of the services as a nurse during World War II. I felt so proud of her.

So, I'm now left with Clara and her antics. She was, more or less, in the same situation as I was in staying around home for a while. Her mother and father were both crippled so it wasn't easy for them to get around. Her older sister, Lillian, was in poor health. I can only imagine that, because her two older brothers were working, she was needed to help in the home. Her brother, Claude, like my brother, Walter, was still in school. Clara and I often went bike riding, especially on Sundays. We would even go as far as Bessacarr and surprise Father. We went to see the Doncaster Rovers' soccer team play but neither of us knew what its colors were. Then one Saturday afternoon we decided, on the spur of the moment, to go to Bullar's Dance Studio. This was merely out of curiosity. It was inexpensive and you only paid extra if you wanted private lessons. We just hung around to get the gist of the lessons and ended up dancing with each other.

Apart from fooling around at some of the dances following the Whist drives, I had never done any dancing. The fact that I was now wearing shoes all the time made it seem feasible and I couldn't wait to go again. My main concern, as usual, was my legs. I wasn't so self-conscious anymore because my legs were actually much straighter, but by no means perfect. I still felt the need to hide them but I really loved this ballroom dancing and took to it like a duck to water. Of course, I mostly danced with girls except when it was ladies choice, but what young man would choose to dance with a shrimp, or "short stuff" as I was now affectionately called. By now, I could care less as dancing became my real cup of tea and I couldn't get enough of it. I think it was almost as good for my legs as the cycling was or maybe it was just my wishful thinking. Clara was not so enthusiastic and I ended up going alone and dancing with girls who didn't do any better than I, when it came to partners.

I stayed home and didn't go to the lessons when the weather got too cold, but I started saving like mad to buy a couple of new dresses, and my first pair of high heels. I did a lot of knitting and also helped Mother with orders for men's golfing socks which were worn with the popular plus fours. I was a whiz at Argyle and Fair Isle patterns. Mother was a whiz when it came to shaping feet. So, we helped each other. We both excelled in making white, silk scarves which was the style worn by the R.A.F. officers. Although they were easy to make and very smart looking, they were also very time consuming and the demand was always more than we could supply.

Just before Christmas, Father came home from Bessacarr and asked if I would care to do a paper route for about six weeks. The news agent at Cantley needed someone until the regular carrier came back after an accident. That's when I realized my mistake in cycling to Bessacarr. Father figured, if I could ride that far, I could make it to Cantley which was only three miles. I was angry at first, but he said he would help me the first week until I knew my way around. He was sure I could use the money, which was true.

"No businessman can be expected to go to his office without first reading his moring paper," said Father.

Father was so convincing, so I agreed.

Cantley was a suburban district where the residents were mostly upper class. The large homes had such long driveways and I had to take the papers up to their front doors. I will never forget those cold, frosty mornings when I had to be up by 5:30 a.m. in order to cycle the three miles before starting the deliveries. To make matters worse, there were times when the fog would suddenly appear, and even with a light on my bicycle, it was almost impossible to see. These times were scary. Why on earth did I take this job, especially before daylight? I was afraid of the dark and known by all as a small, delicate one. I wonder how Amy Johnson would have tackled this? I know, of course, there is no comparison to her solo flight but I think I deserved a medal.

I never let on to Father until much later, but before the six weeks were up I was actually enjoying myself. The bad parts were that I had to get up so early without any fire, and of course the darkness. I was always glad to see the daylight. There was something about being in the open air when the light slowly broke through with birds singing as they flitted around looking for food.

As I rode home each day on the Great North Road, with the race course on one side and the Doncaster Rovers' soccer field on the other, I felt a sort of satisfaction. I had actually helped someone out, if only for a short time, as well as helping myself with more exercise.

When the racing season came around again, I did my duties to help as usual. The building contracts were coming to an end in our area which meant that the betting business would also be slowing down soon.

The elementary school was already finished except for a lot of clean up work so this still meant plenty of work for Father. On top of that, he was given a contract to clean the school windows on a regular basis. He eventually had to hire a couple of strong boys to help him with the higher windows, because he was so short.

Anyway, the betting business was slowing down, and we all knew it would come to an end, sooner or later. For the time being, if Lucie would cover for me once in a while, I would go to my dancing on Saturday afternoons.

I had developed a crush on one of the apprentice jockeys whose name was Alf Taylor. He was at least six years older than I was and I'm sure that Lucie and Elsie had previously been on a date with him. He was so handsome and also a very nice person. His home was in West Hartlepool. Mother always made him feel welcome, I think she was secretly hoping one of us would end up with him. I also had a crush on a young man who worked in a food store downtown whose name was Bernard Patrick, but that's all it amounted to. Alf Taylor was sent far away to ride in Saratoga Springs, New York and we didn't see him again for a very long time, although he wrote to me occasionally. I had managed to have a few dates by the time I reached seventeen. I remember Elsie giving me all kinds of advice and really watching over me. She had no need to worry, I had not been very impressed so far. I also think I wasn't quite mature enough, and the fact that I was so short didn't help me. I looked so young.

I only wish Elsie had taken some of her own advice and not plunged into marriage so soon. Unfortunately, it didn't work out well at all. I felt so sorry for her because she deserved much better. She was a lot like Father, strong willed, outspoken, and very honest.

So, now it was just Walter and me left at home. He was big enough to help Father with some of the odd jobs but he was never called on to help with the horse racing.

My friend Clara had finally gone into the work force, but it wasn't too long before she married a professional soccer player and we didn't see much of her after that.

Elsie and her husband, Hubert Dews, and Lucie and Eric lived close by. So, we still saw a lot of them; especially at meal times. It was only on Saturdays that Father needed help with the racing these days and we girls were available when it was necessary.

Elsie still did Mother's grocery shopping for a while and I knew I would inherit that job before too long. The only time I saw Mother buy food was when she went on her annual shopping spree and we were all there to help her. The rest of the year it was left to us. This was a real thorn in our sides as she was so fastidious, she refused to purchase everything at one stop so neither could we.

We lived in the Hyde Park district where there were quite a few small shops, and even when we were still in school, there wasn't a day that we didn't have to go there as soon as we got home. What made it worse still is that we often had to take items back because they weren't fresh or for some other reason. I remember we had to go to a certain shop just for yeast only. This was a creepy, dark place where a bell tinkled as the door opened and a little, old woman with one big tooth and scraggly hair would appear. She reminded me of a character from a Dicken's novel.

Then, there was Miss Hutchinson, who, incidentally, was the spinster sister of Father's builder friend. She supposedly had the best bacon for sale, but many times we were sent right back with it. Either it was too fat or, on occasion, there were maggots in it. This wasn't really surprising because there was little refrigeration those days.

Elsie seemed to do better at the downtown stores than I, but she had strict orders to bring Danish butter, Cheshire cheese and Australian dried fruits for making scones. Woe betide if the fish came from anywhere but Birkenshaw's. However, we all agreed the worst was going to the butcher shop. The sides of beef, lamb and pork were hung in plain sight and one could choose any cut or pick from a variety of already cut pieces. Try as we might, we never seemed to pick the right piece of meat.

Lucky for us, the produce was sold by hawkers who came around to the houses two or three times a week. They also had wild rabbits which were still in their skins.

I still wonder about the fact that Mother never thought she was being unreasonable. We often suggested she do the shopping herself on weekends and leave the housework for us to do, but that was definitely out of the question. If I had to look for a fault in her, the shopping would be the only one, and I have to confess, some of that fault passed on to me. I am accused almost daily of being too picky when it comes to food.

As for Father, I still have a lot more to tell about him but so far his good points have more than outweighed any mistakes he may have made.

The Courtship

The year 1933 started out rather slowly, but for me it turned out to be a most memorable one. I met a young man, Philip, who eventually became the love of my life. He had recently moved to Doncaster from Burton-On-Trent in Staffordshire. He was doing part of his apprenticeship in the baking industry at the Danum Bakery where Lucie's husband, Eric, was employed.

Sometime in March, Lucie told me she had met this young man. She and Eric were going to a staff dinner and dance on April 5th and they invited Philip to go along with them. He asked Lucie if she had a sister who might like to go as his date. So when she asked me, I agreed to go. I felt a little nervous at first, even though it wasn't really a blind date. Lucie told me a little about him which helped somewhat. As the time drew closer, I was actually looking forward to my very first dinner and dance.

I decided to wear my new dress. It wasn't a formal, but luckily, I had not yet shortened it as I had to do with all the dresses I bought so it was the right length for the occasion. I was able to dress it up a little with a few accessories. Of course, I would wear my high heels.

This affair took place at the Bentley Pavilion, which is situated at the edge of a small boating lake. Bentley is a suburb just outside of Doncaster.

Finally the big day came. It was on a Wednesday and when we arrived at the pavilion, Philip was waiting for us along with three of his friends and their girl friends. After we were introduced, we took our places at the tables. Sitting right next to Philip for dinner gave me a chance to observe him at close range.

Philip certainly didn't fit the description Lucie had given me. I thought he was quite good looking, even with a prominent nose. His eyes were blue-grey and his hair a medium brown and slightly wavy. During the dinner my attention was focused on his beautiful hands. They looked like the hands of an artist. Most of all they were so noticeably clean, especially his fingernails.

We talked about his work and he explained he had chosen the Danum Bakery because it was a reputable firm and would pay part of his tuition to go to evening classes at the local technical college for baking. Of course, he had to prove that he had the potential to become a master baker and confectioner before he would be hired.

When dinner was over, we took a stroll outside until the band set up for the dance. I remember so vividly that there were several exits which opened onto small bridges spanning part of the lake. Philip told me he usually went dancing on Saturday nights to the same studio that I went to on Saturday afternoons so I knew then he was probably quite a good dancer.

When we heard the music start, we wound our way through the crowd and onto the center of the floor. To say, at this moment, that I was excited is putting it mildly. When he put his arm around me, as we started to dance, it felt wonderful. I knew immediately that I really liked this young man. The more we danced, the more I looked forward to feeling the touch of his hand on mine.

During the interval, we mingled with his friends and I learned they were all going to evening classes at the same college so they had much in common.

After we changed partners and Philip danced with their girl friends, it became clear to me these young men were real good friends. I really enjoyed being part of the group.

I was wishing this night could go on forever. I was having such a good time. Lucie and Eric weren't very interested in dancing so they did very little and were content to sit around and visit with their friends.

As the evening drew to its close, we went outside one more time. We sat down on a little bridge and the reflection of the moon was on the lake, giving a romantic atmosphere to the late night air. Philip put his arm around me, bent over and gave me a very gentle kiss which I will always remember. I just simply melted, and to my surprise and joy, he asked me for a date to go dancing the following weekend. Needless to say, I was thrilled beyond words and when we went back to the dance floor for the last waltz they were playing the song, "It's Three O'clock in the Morning," and my heart just sang the words that I knew so well. It was the end of a perfect evening.

At that time, Philip was living with relatives across town, so after bidding each other good night, I left with Lucie and Eric. I know I got into the taxi, but I actually rode all the way home on cloud nine and kept pinching myself to make sure this was really happening and that I was going to see him again.

During the following week, I went about my usual routine and tried not to dwell on our upcoming date. I was afraid to be too optimistic in case Philip might have changed his mind, and I didn't want to face that kind of let-down. I'm sure it was obvious to my family that I was in a state of elation but I wanted to keep them guessing so I didn't tell them about the date until the day before.

Since Philip wasn't acquainted with the town, we arranged to meet at Bullar's Dance Studio. I was so looking forward to this second meeting with him and when I saw him waiting for me my heart skipped a beat and then starting pounding like a drum.

I had only been to the afternoon dance sessions before, so I was pleasantly surprised to see more young couples at this night session. There was also a much bigger and better band than at the afternoon sessions. I felt rather important knowing I had my own partner and that my high heels gave me somewhat of a lift as Philip was almost one foot taller than me.

This evening turned out equally as good, if not better, than the first one. There were just the two of us. We danced almost every dance, and we had so much to talk about. It didn't take long to find Philip had a great sense of humour.

On our way home, walking arm in arm, we did as most English people do, we bought fish and chips wrapped in the traditional newspaper. We put salt and malt vinegar on them and ate them with our fingers. Those days it was the equivalent of today's American hamburger and fries and just as cheap. To me it was just as scrumptious as the dinner at the dance the week before.

Our home was a two story, brick house and the end one of four attached to each other. We had the advantage of an alley which separated us from the next row of four. When we got there, I was quick to point out a warm section on the side of the house where the fireplace was situated just inside in the living room where my sisters used to lean against the wall with their boy friends on many a cold night. Mother, always knowing they were there, would signal for them to come in by a tap of the poker at the back of the fire grate. Philip thought that was funny and suggested we keep the ritual going, but I was anxious for him to meet Mother, so we went inside.

I knew right away that she liked him. She made tea and brought out her "rough and ready" cake which, in later years, Philip always teased her about by saying it was rough all right and that you had to be ready for it.

Dad wasn't home that night. He had recently gotten a job, just for Saturdays, as a night watchman at the Danum Bakery. He was able to take his Alsatian dog with him for company, and he held that job for many years.

When I finally went to bed, I couldn't sleep for thinking that just over a week ago I was this person of no consequence whatsoever and now I felt as though I had been completely transformed, almost like magic. I didn't think it was possible to feel so happy and more mature at the same time. How could everything have change so quickly? Could it have been because this nice young man had suddenly come into my life?

Philip had much more schooling than I had, and considering he was only two months older, it was obvious he was beyond compare. I was definitely in awe of him. However, our friendship grew over the next few months. We couldn't always go dancing or to a movie because of the lack of funds so we would go to the many, nice parks in our area. On Sunday afternoons there were free brass band concerts, or we would go for walks to Sandle Beat woods. Philip enjoyed this, having grown up in a small village in the country. I noticed his interest in birds and their nesting. He knew exactly where to look for them. He told me one of his hobbies was painting these birds and all sorts of wild flowers. He also liked to go fishing and swimming in the River Trent near his home.

I envied his enthusiasm for his work, simply because I was always held back due to one thing or another. I felt there was a certain prestige in having a job, and I kept telling myself, "When the racing business is ended, my day will come." But what on earth would I do? I didn't have any real skills. How I wished I had taken Dad's advice and gone to high school. On the other hand, I might never have met Philip which was a good stroke of fate.

Due to his weekend job, it was quite a while before Dad actually met Philip, but apparently he had caught a glimpse of him one day at the bakery. All he said to me was, "I'll tell you this much, Genty, that young man's a real worker." It was then I remember I started complaining about wanting a real job and Dad said, "You were cut out to be a genteel lady, but you're having a bit of bad luck." Thus, my pet name of "*Genty*" stuck to me in reference to Genteel.

We had heard a lot from Philip about his aunt and uncle with whom he stayed and one day he took me to see them. Aunt Alice, his mother's sister and her husband, Fred Wells, owned a wholesale and retail fruit and vegetable business. In return for his room and board, Philip helped them whenever he possibly could. They had a retail shop where they lived and also operated three stands in the Doncaster Market Place on

Tuesdays, Fridays, and Saturdays. One stand was for flowers only and was always a beautiful sight to behold. They were just as particular in arranging their bouquets as they were with their produce. Everything was of the best quality. Most of the flowers were grown locally, but Uncle Fred used to drive his lorry way down south to Ipswich where he bought most of his produce.

He told me that some people made a living by growing a certain type of ivy which produced extra large leaves. These leaves were made to shine and then sold for the purpose of placing one under each apple, orange, or pear at the market place. This made the fruit look more attractive on the display tables. There was a lot of competition in the market place so it was a matter of how appealing and how fresh the produce looked to the prospective buyer.

Uncle Fred was a quiet, unassuming man. He knew the business very well so he made a good living. He also helped his widowed sister who was in the same business by doing all the buying for her. He also did the buying for several other younger people to get them started. It was very interesting to walk around and hear the sales people, many of them farmers, shouting out their wares.

Aunt Alice was a nice little lady with auburn hair. She had a happy twinkle in her eyes and always appeared so pleasant and even tempered. I'm sure she was a big asset to their business. They were both well respected by all the market people.

When I got to know her better, I found she was a great cook. She told me she was trained to cook when she was in the service of a Gentry household in the country. These particular family members were descendants of the famous British statesman and Prime Minister, Sir Robert (Bobby) Peel. It was he who reorganized the London police force and thus the policeman got the name--"*Bobby.*"

If I'm not mistaken, I think Aunt Alice told me that one of the gentlemen in this household was married to the famous

British actress, Beatrice Lillie. She felt very proud to have cooked for these celebrities.

As the racing season came to a close that year and winter was almost upon us, I took on Mother's downtown shopping. I didn't mind this now because it gave me the opportunity to stroll around the market and see my new-found friends, and Philip. He got off work at noon on Saturday's and then went over to help at the market the rest of the afternoon. He was kept busy replenishing the produce as fast as it was sold. Being artistic, he was able to arrange everything to the best advantage. I decided to go on Tuesday the following week and offered to help in any capacity and was soon put to work. I didn't want any pay. I just wanted to feel useful.

Aunt Alice always patronized other market people so she put me in charge of doing all her personal shopping such as butter and eggs, jams and jellies, an occasional home baked item from the farmers wives, and sandwiches for lunch. This all saved her a great deal of time. I also did their banking before closing, 3:00 p.m. those days, so I was feeling somewhat pleased with myself. Usually, by the time their day was ended, things had been picked over and the selection was gone. When it was time for the market to close, I helped to load up whatever was left which they would sell in their shop at home in the next few days. Uncle Fred would drive down to Ipswich for more supplies for the weekend. They filled my basket with fruits and vegetables to take home which my mother gratefully accepted.

I was told I could help whenever it suited me, so I took their offer and went on Tuesdays and Fridays. As it got closer to Christmas, they were extra busy so I was able to serve some of the customers. I was really enjoying this change. I actually had a job of sorts. Even though I wasn't paid in cash, the fringe benefits were enough for me. I felt like I was really stepping out of my shell and, at the same time, I met a lot of interesting people from all walks of life.

I was really looking forward to the holiday season until Philip told me he had decided to go home to Burton-on-Trent to spend Christmas with his parents as he felt he had neglected them somewhat. It wasn't easy for him to get away but he hadn't seen them for almost a year.

I suddenly felt a sense of doubt. Would he be coming back or would he have a change of plans? I wondered if there was a girl there? He hadn't spoken of anyone special. I kept telling myself he wouldn't just leave without letting his employer know of his intentions. He would only be gone over the long weekend, but I still couldn't help feeling a little uneasy, even before he left.

We had our usual Christmas at home. I helped Aunt Alice on the day before so she gave me a lot of special things such as: Jaffa oranges, tangerines, pomegranates, and a box of dried fruits, dates, figs, apricots, and fancy nuts. Up to this time in my life I have always managed to get those dried fruits that we enjoyed so much. I think it's a reminder of my association with Aunt Alice and Uncle Fred at Christmas time and it makes me feel a little sentimental.

When Philip came home, I didn't get to see him until the following weekend. We had planned that, all being well, we would go to a New Year's Eve dance, and sure enough, he came to our home about 7 o'clock that evening where I was waiting in suspense. I was so happy to see him that I had a hard time holding back a few tears of joy, while at the same time I was feeling a little guilty for having any trace of doubt. After spending a few minutes with my mom, we left and he took me to a new place, which in the summer was used for public swimming and in the winter the water was drained and a wooden floor was put down for dancing. It was a huge place, much nicer than the small studio where we were constantly running into each other. There was also an excellent band and many professionals who had plenty of room to show off their dancing skills.

This being a special occasion, there were quite an assortment of fancy pastries for refreshments and party hats and noise makers to celebrate the New Year. This was my first time out for such an event and spending it with Philip made it all the more exciting. I was having a wonderful time. My cup was really running over as Philip kissed me at the stroke of midnight while the band played "Auld Lang Syne."

On the way home, Philip told me all about his Christmas day. His mother had cooked a goose. It was a Christmas box from the farm where she worked as a general helper. His dad worked at a butcher's shop where they had their own abattoir on the premises, so he was involved in most of the slaughtering. The local farmers often called on him, especially around Christmas, to kill and dress a pig for them. He was happy to oblige. He could always use a little extra money. He usually brought home a good pork roast and the pig trotters as an added bonus. Instead of buying him a Christmas gift, his parents gave him some money toward the purchase of a bicycle. He needed one to get to work by 5 a.m. at the bakery.

After the Christmas festivities ended, there was very little to do in the way of entertainment besides Philip was eager to save more money in hopes of getting his bike in the spring. We spent much time listening to music on the wireless or going for long walks whenever the weather permitted it. Then, one Sunday Philip asked Mother if she would allow him to bake something for her, and much to my surprise, she immediately gave him the run of her kitchen. From that day on, he was in all his glory. To say that we were amazed was a great understatement. Every weekend he was content to experiment on something different. We could hardly wait to see what mouth watering morsels he would come up with next. My dad was so impressed that he told Mother to give him a free hand. It was so obvious that Philip knew the trade and was willing to work his head off to better himself. He was not yet 20 years old, but there seemed to be no end to his appetite for perfection. It was magical to watch his techniques.

I never saw such wonderful looking French pastries, petit fours, gateaus, and marzipan goods. His talent seemed to know no bounds. I think this is when my dad realized Philip's full potential and never failed to give him the praise that he so deserved.

My mother was happy with plainer goods, like croissants, sultana scones, and crumpets. However, I can see her now, after Philip had finished cutting out the different shapes of petit fours and before dipping them in fondant, as she would go around picking up all the cuttings and bits of almond paste and then put them aside to enjoy another day.

Another thing comes to mind at a time when he was experimenting with chocolate. He would heat the chocolate and spread it thinly on a piece of cellophane paper. He would then place it on the floor close to the door where it would cool off enough to cut out different shapes.

Poor Mother, the times she forgot it was there and when a knock came on the door she stepped onto the chocolate which made her feel bad. Philip never complained because he was so thankful for all of the encouragement he was given, even in such a small kitchen with a very small gas oven.

In the meantime, he managed to get his new bicycle and took time out for a little recreation. We would ride together on Sundays, maybe to Dad's estate at Bessacarr or around the racecourse which was a popular place for sweethearts those days. It was here, one day, that we stopped and sat down on the grass and, for the first time, he told me that he loved me. I, in turn, told him that I loved him very much too.

Later that year, he asked my parents if it was all right for me to go with him to spend Christmas at his home and, after some gentle persuading, they agreed to let me go.

The next time we went dancing, Philip asked me to sit down because he had something to tell me. He looked serious, so I knew it was important. It seems he had recently written to a firm through the British Baker's Magazine in reference to a job and this firm was interested enough to grant him an interview after Christmas. I asked him right away if he was serious about moving on and he said he was looking for more experience and hoped I would understand. My heart was sinking, but I told him he must do what was best for himself. I also said I wouldn't want to visit his parents this Christmas, maybe some other time. I was feeling too sad at the thought of the possibility of his leaving Doncaster so I was very happy when he decided to not go home until after his interview in January.

We were still in the betting business although we knew Dad was losing interest. We girls, as well as Mother, were hoping this would be the last season. When it was over, I immediately went to the market place. I knew I had to stay busy in order to keep from being depressed. Of course, Philip hadn't been for the interview, yet, but somehow we all knew he would have no problem.

Christmas week arrived before we knew it. The market was open every day and I worked the whole time. Philip had to work longer at the bakery on Christmas Eve so I didn't see him until later that evening. He showed up at my home with extra Christmas goodies that I was hardly able to fit into my basket, plus a beautiful bouquet of greenhouse chrysanthemums for my mother which made her feel very special. Dad had to work that night which left my brother to stay with Mother, so she was pleased that we were there and Walter was glad to have Philip's company for a change.

We had a real jolly evening roasting chestnuts, eating Mother's mince tarts, and sipping blackberry wine. Later the familiar sound of carol singers rang in the crisp night air. They went around in groups until almost midnight. I felt sorry to have to send Phil home. He was so tired, but he had promised to have Christmas dinner with Aunt Alice and Uncle Fred and at least he could sleep in at their home. They didn't have any family so they were looking forward to him being there. I learned later that they were fun to be with, and Aunt Alice's cooking was out of this world. Uncle Fred seemed to open up, and I saw a new side to him. He could be quite funny.

I knew that Philip had a sense of humour, but it really came to light that Christmas day when I mentioned being sorry about not meeting his family.

He just said, "You wouldn't want to see my brother anyway because he's a freak."

I asked, "What is wrong with him."

He replied, "He's got three feet."

By this time I was a little suspicious and I said, "Are you kidding me?"

"Oh no!" he answered. "I received a letter from my mother the other day and she said you wouldn't recognize your brother, he's grown another foot." If he was trying to keep my spirits up, he certainly succeeded that day.

About two weeks later he went for the interview, and sure enough, he got the job. It was at a place called Cannock Chase which was about 95 miles away but to me it might just as well been 1,000, especially those days. The main attraction for Philip was that they had an excellent chocolatier at this firm, and they also did catering so Philip was already looking forward to this new challenge. Anyway, he didn't have to start until mid March so we had a little more time together.

The first Saturday afternoon in March he said we were going shopping and, much to my surprise, he stopped in front of Thompson's Jewelers downtown. In one particular section of the window there was an array of rings with a sign that read, "Forfeited Pledges." These rings looked just like new but obviously they had been pawned at some time and not been redeemed. Philip asked me if I would mind having a ring that had been worn by someone else because that was all that he could afford. He had never hinted about giving me a ring, so I was speechless. He just led me into the store and asked to look at the tray of rings.

The only one that fit my finger was a size 5 gold ring with 3 tiny diamonds. I told him I liked that one because it was tiny like me. I would look out of place with a big stone so that was it. He put it on my finger in the store and gave me a big hug and a kiss and then he said, "Now we are officially engaged."

We went home to spend the rest of the day with my mother. We wanted her to be the first to know about the ring. She took my left hand and placed it in Philip's right hand and said, "Bless you both and good luck." I could tell she was very pleased. We had tea, and of course, out came the rough and ready cake. Because of the occasion, we had a drink of port wine instead of the usual home-made wine. Mother was doing her best to make the evening special and I tried hard to put on a happy face, even though I was feeling sad inside. When it was time for Philip to leave, I went outside with him. As usual, I cuddled up inside his coat and we leaned against the warm, brick wall. While doing a little smooching, I realized I was going to miss these times. I also knew that little ring was very precious to me.

A week later Philip was gone, and I had no idea when I would see him again. He promised to write, but I knew he would be busy with his new job and finding a place to stay. I had to be patient. About ten days later my first letter arrived. It was full of excitement about his work. He sounded very much at ease and full of praise for his fellow workers. They were so friendly, but most of all he was impressed with the high quality of the bakery goods. He then told me he understood my feelings about his leaving because he felt the same way. Not only did he miss me, but also my parents because they had always been so good to him, as also was Aunt Alice and Uncle Fred. It was at this time he told me they had lent him the money to buy my ring but he had left his bicycle with them for collateral. He didn't want to tell me at the time in case I wouldn't understand, and he did want us to become engaged before he left. He agreed to pay back the money as soon as possible so that Uncle Fred could send his bicycle to him by train.

The rest of his letter was full of loving endearments which really warmed my heart. I read it over and over again, especially the part where he said it may take a long time, but hopefully someday he would be in a position for us to get married. I accepted the fact there and then that this could be a long courtship by mail, but somehow, I would live through it. I had already resigned myself to the fact that I wasn't going to see much of him. That was the hardest part.

Anyway, two months and many letters later, I had a wonderful surprise. One Saturday afternoon I went to answer a knock on the door and there stood Philip with a pack on his back, and his bicycle parked in the yard. I was thrilled beyond words and couldn't get into his arms fast enough. When the shock wore off, he told me he had planned this trip for some time but had only got his bicycle a couple of days ago. He was very tired but he said it was well worth it just to see the look of surprise on my face. He explained that he didn't ride all the 95 miles, he was lucky enough to get a ride with a lorry (truck) driver the last half of the way.

I had just helped Philip off with his back pack when Mother came in the kitchen to see what all the excitement was about. He opened the pack and handed me a cake box so I opened it and there, wrapped so carefully, was a beautiful chocolate Easter egg. My name was on the egg surrounded by crystallized purple sugar violets. It was so pretty. He hadn't taken long to learn from the chocolatier. I felt so proud and very special.

Mother was also happy to get a nice assortment of bakery goodies. She wouldn't have to bake again for a while. Of course, it went without saying, my brother Walter could not wait to sample such goodies. He was beginning to like Philip more and more, and they really did become very good friends for many years to come.

The surprise visit was wonderful but having to say good-bye the next day was very tearful. Shakespeare said it perfectly when he wrote, "Parting is such sweet sorrow." However, Philip promised to come again in a month's time but in between time he would go to visit his parents for a weekend. Their home was only half the distance away.

While the time seemed to drag for me, it was really flying for Philip. He was working so hard, yet, he found time to write. I was always impressed by the way he could express himself, not only about his love for me but the way he talked about his work which was very important to him. He often wrote a few lines in shorthand and then would say, "For your eyes only." I would have to wait until I saw him again so that he could translate the message. He had learned both shorthand and typing in school.

He was as good as his word and came again to see me on his bicycle. This time he told me it would be a while before his next visit. Apparently, he and another young fellow worker were chosen to represent their firm in international competition for pastry cooks, to be held in London at the end of September and this would require much preparatory work.

It would also give Philip a real opportunity to shine. He had done well in regional competition, but this was his first entry in International. He was excited at the possibilities it could hold for him, yet, in his excitement, he remained as cool as a cucumber while I was always so nervous. I often wished some of his self confidence would rub off onto me.

I never did see him get frustrated over anything but I do remember, just after we first met, he told me it had been his ambition to have a career in the British Navy. He knew it was difficult to get in, especially in peace time, because the exams were so rigidly precise so he applied for all the forms before he left school in order to get a head start. He passed everything, with flying colors except the physical. His local doctor wouldn't pass him. This was very frustrating for him, and it took him a long time to get over his disappointment.

Getting back to the competition, he came to see me as soon as it was over, and this time he came on a brand new motor bike. I couldn't believe my eyes. It was a beautiful machine and he was so proud of it. He had traded in his good racing bicycle and was paying the remainder on credit. He finally got around to telling us that he and his co-worker had done very well in the competition. They won several awards, including two first places, and their firm got a special award for producing a new sweet bread. This was a dark, malt fruit loaf called Sinutro.

Phil stressed the fact that, even though it was easier now to travel on his motor bike, it would depend mostly on the weather conditions. There was always fog to contend with and I accepted that without any misgivings. I didn't want him to court any danger so it was agreed he would spend that Christmas with his parents.

We only had about six weeks of horse racing left, and Dad finally made up his mind that this would be the last year, for which we were all truly thankful. When I told Aunt Alice, she said I could work for her in their home shop. I would be company for her when Uncle Fred went on his buying trips, and I would also get paid.

I had just gotten started nicely into my new venture about the first week in December when one Sunday evening I heard the sound of Philip's motor bike. I was at the back door in a flash and got a scare when I saw his right hand all bandaged. I thought he had been in an accident. However, he soon proceeded to tell us that he had cut his middle finger at work. Apparently, blood poisoning had set in and was spreading through his hand. When he got in the house, he sat down and passed out. I thanked God for my mother that night as she stayed up with him and bathed his hand constantly. It had swollen almost to the size of a boxing glove, and he was in much pain. I went with him early the next morning to the doctor's office and he was told to go straight to the infirmary so they could remove the finger, or he could lose his arm.

This ended up being a dragged out affair. He didn't lose his finger, but they did lance it to let the poison out and when the swelling went down they put a cast on. Unfortunately, it wasn't set right so he ended up with necrosis of the bone. As a result of this, his finger was permanently stiff and when he made a fist the finger just protruded out. This bothered him at first, knowing his right hand was his main tool for his trade, but somehow he got used to it, and eventually it never seemed to bother him except for the disfigurement.

Philip was given regular wages for the six weeks he was off work. He stayed with us during that time so my mother acted as his nurse. I was so determined to start out 1936, by seeking some kind of work. I searched the "wanted" ads and went from store to store, but of course, I didn't get very far for lack of experience. I even put my name down in the movie theatres, but the only thing I managed to do during the whole month of January was take care of my niece, Jean. Lucie had given birth to another baby girl, Beryl, a month earlier. Then, on January 8, Elsie had a baby girl, Elizabeth Ann. We called her Betty. I was 21 on January 22, and was feeling somewhat downcast because I was not earning any money, except for the small amount at the market.

Barton-Under-Needwood

Toward the end of March, Philip was entitled to a week vacation and he suggested I forget about work, for the time being. Since we had been engaged for a year, he wanted me to meet his parents. He planned for us to spend a week with them and celebrate the third anniversary of our first date on April 5. It didn't cost me anything because he took me and brought me back on his motor bike and I shared his sister's bedroom. After getting the OK from my parents, we set out early one Sunday morning. It was quite cold so I wrapped up well and my small suitcase was strapped to the carrier behind me. As we got well on the way, it started to warm up and I was enjoying the ride. I could understand Philip's liking this machine. I felt as free as a bird. I hadn't seen so much of the countryside before so we stopped from time to time to take in the beautiful scenery of the Yorkshire dales, through Nottingham into Derbyshire, and finally to Burton-on-Trent in Staffordshire where they make all the beer. All this, yet, we had only covered about 70 miles. We had about five miles more before we would come to the small village of Barton-Under-Needwood. As we drove down the main street, we passed St. James Church, which at that time was almost 500 years old. Philip told me he used to attend there three times every Sunday to sing in the choir.

We turned onto Wales Lane where his home was, and I began to feel a little nervous. What kind of an impression would I make on these people? Philip, sensing my fears, gave my hand a squeeze and told me not to worry.

That Sunday afternoon was the most I saw of Philip's parents, Fred and Hannah Richardson. They made me feel welcome and had a good dinner waiting for us. Philip definitely had his mother's features. She was a lot like Aunt Alice with her auburn hair. His dad was a small, thin man who suffered from bronchial asthma. His sister, Edith, was nineteen and was working as a cook at a large estate in the village. His twelve year old brother, Albert, was still in school. Philip was actually born in another village called Hanbury about eight miles away, but this was where he grew up and went to school. He wanted me to see everything, and in doing so, we walked for miles through the fields, meadows, and farm lands. We picked mushrooms at the crack of dawn. When I first spotted one, I was so excited I felt like I had struck oil. At the same time, I wasn't so excited when in the misty fog I encountered a cow a little too close for comfort.

Philip said, "I never saw you move so fast." He also told me that we were actually trespassing on the farmer's property, and it reminded him of when he was still in school.

He used to go every morning, gather as many mushrooms as he could carry and then go to the large estates and sell them to the cooks. This was working very well for him until one day this particular farmer was riding through the village on his horse and buggy and spotted Philip walking home from school. Without any warning, he pulled the buggy close to the side of the road, picked up his horse whip with a long thin lash, and cracked it hard toward Philip catching the back of his legs. Then, he said, "Let that be a lesson to you. Keep out of my field." So, the business venture was short lived.

We visited all the little stores, the post office, and the news agency run by two old ladies. They were so happy to see Philip. He had delivered papers for them for many years. They had missed him but were glad to know of his making a name for himself in the baking trade.

This country life was so peaceful to me and everyone, including his family, had a sense of humour. Not funny like Philip's, but a pleasant way of expressing themselves, and of course, a different dialect which sounded funny to me. I couldn't always understand it. I was a true Yorkshire girl, and much of my accent became noticeable in Philip when he started to pick up some of my Yorkshire slang.

It was easy to tell that he didn't or never did like the idea of his mother going out to work, and I'm sure his dad felt the same way. Not so much that she worked 3 1/2 days a week at the farm close by, but because it didn't stop there. She brought all their mending and sewing home, and on top of that, she made leather gloves, and some of her own clothes. She was a good seamstress. She did make a point of going to the Saturday night dances at the Barton Grange Hall but the rest of the week you could tell she was so tired. Sometimes she would fall asleep over the sewing.

One night, after we were all in bed, I heard a knock on the door and someone softly calling, "Hannah." This woke me up and I nudged Edith.

Then I heard Hannah say, "I'll be right down, Mr. Ball." Edith explained that Mr. Ball was the local undertaker and Hannah was available at all times to help him wash and lay out the body regardless of who it was.

I lay awake all that night thinking of all the work that Philip's mother did and asking myself what kind of an excuse for a housewife would she think I would make for her son. Until I met him, I had led such a sheltered life, and to make matters worse, Edith told me at one of our bedroom girl talks that her mother at one time had a girl picked out for Philip. This girl was selected not because of her good looks but because she was a good worker. But not to worry, our Phil didn't like her anyway. Everyone in the family called him "our Phil" so I adopted the shorter term and called him Phil. I was never able to persuade my family to call him anything but Philip.

Before we left to go back to Doncaster, his sister, knowing I was anxious to get some work, remarked casually that it was too bad I didn't live there because there were plenty of opportunities in domestic service. She gave me the names of two places to contact if I was interested, which I was, but Phil didn't like the idea at all. However, when I pointed out the advantage of getting room and board, plus wages, he softened a little. He did have a point when he reminded me it wasn't just as easy as doing housework. There were all the rules and regulations that go along with being in service and could I handle being away from home at such short notice?

I figured, if we got married, I certainly wouldn't have any qualms about leaving home, so why now? At that point I could hear my dad once again saying, "Never let it be said your Mother bred a jibber." So, I decided to strike while the iron was hot and ask Phil to take me the next morning on our way out of Barton-Under-Needwood to one place in question.

This large estate was called The Dower House and was just a short distance from the main road. Mr. and Mrs. Robinson, who owned it, were also owners of one of the breweries in Burton-On-Trent. When I asked Mrs. Robinson about the job, she informed me it was only temporary but, under the circumstances, she was willing to hire me without the usual references. I told her I had to go home, but I would be back in one week. I wasn't so sure about something temporary, but at least, if I didn't like it then it would be easier for me to leave. I also thought my prompt action would make an impression on Phil's mother, and that, at least, I might see more of him too. Anyway, he took me home and said he would come back for me the following weekend. During that week, I met with my sisters who, although they had only had a short time of live-in service, were full of advice. I think they were trying to scare me.

I gathered my few clothes together. I really didn't need much because I would be wearing a maid's uniform. To pass the time I thought I would do something for Phil. I bought some off-white linen to make a small pennant on which I traced the word "Sinutro", the name of the now famous malt loaf. Then, I embroidered the name with bright red silk thread, and it turned out great. I put a thin stick through the end so that Phil could attach it to the front wheel of his motor bike. He was pleasantly surprised and couldn't wait to see it flying in the wind.

He arrived on the Saturday afternoon, and we left early on Sunday morning. Both my mother and dad wished me luck but said not to worry if it didn't work out. Mother packed us a lunch, and being such a beautiful day, we picked a nice spot to stop because we did not know when we would see each other again.

Well, I did work for the Robinson Family, but my stay this time was short lived, about three months. I say, "this time" because I was employed by them a few years later. However, right now the young lady whose place I was taking returned after her leave of absence due to illness in her family.

I didn't see much of Mr. Robinson. He was gone most of the day, but Mrs. Robinson was a very kind, genteel lady and did her best not to make me feel intimidated by her or the sudden change in my life style. Their teenage daughter, whom I addressed as Miss Mavis, was in school, but I did see her from time to time. I have to be honest and say that my first night in this beautiful country estate was the loneliest night of my life, and the silence was almost deafening. The next morning I was up at 6 a.m. and ready for my first duties at 7 a.m. My fears were soon put to rest when I met Nancy, the upstairs maid.

Mrs. Robinson took time to outline my schedule for the day and showed me how to set the dining room table for each meal and how I would serve the food. I washed the dishes, glassware, silver, and china in that order. The dirty pots and pans were cleaned separately in the scullery sink.

Then, came the usual housework of using the vacuum cleaner, dusting, taking out the ashes from the fireplaces, etc. When I got a lull in the afternoon, I had to polish the silver and/or the brassware. It took a little time, but I did manage to get into a routine. It seemed I had just reached that point when I had to leave.

I think my only regret was not seeing enough of Phil. I had an afternoon and evening off until 10 p.m. but this was during the week so I was lucky if I saw him briefly on weekends. I had every other Saturday evening off from 6 to 10 p.m.

I did have some pleasant memories though. Miss Mavis was a lovely girl with blonde hair, blue eyes, dimples, and an infectious laugh. I'm often reminded of her, through one of my grand-daughters when she speaks or laughs. It is like she has a bubble in her voice. When I went about my duties, there were times I could hear this beautiful music, and I would peek into the room and see Miss Mavis sitting at the piano. I often praised her for this until I found out that she was just playing a joke on me. She was just sitting before a player piano. She thought that was funny.

All day Friday and half a day Saturday we had the company of a chore lady. She did the rough work like scrubbing the kitchen and scullery floors, the front entrance, and the steps. Mrs. Ames was a jolly person with a large family. When she joined us for lunch, she had plenty to talk about, and by coincidence, her oldest son was a good friend of Phil's. They had gone to school together.

I must not forget the gardener. He was a small man named Jesse. He looked a little odd to some people because he had a glass eye. We were given the same good food as the household, and Jesse always sat at our kitchen table for lunch. Nancy told me he wasn't always welcomed by some of the previous help because of his looks. This made me feel sad because he was such a nice, quiet man. When people showed him a little compassion, he would do anything for them.
This incident brings to mind a serious side of Phil. He had a great deal of compassion for anyone who had an affliction of any kind. Woe betide anyone if he found them guilty of taunting such a person.

It so happened that one of his friends that I met on our first date, whose name was Les Emmerson, had crossed eyes so he had to wear thick eye glasses. Phil told me that Les was often subjected to ridicule and verbal abuse by some of the workers so he set out to do something about it. A few of them got together and came up with schemes to embarrass the offenders. The friends came up with the ideas, but Les had to carry them out and the things they did were hilarious. I can still laugh when I think about them, but I think Les put an end to it himself when one day the offending parties went to change clothes to go home but none of their clothes were to be found. They had to go home in their work clothes. The next day they discovered their clothes which were all nailed to a high ceiling in one of the store rooms, and I think they finally got the message.

When I left Barton-Under-Needwood, there was nothing else for me to do at the time. Edith promised to let me know if she heard of anything, and I decided to let Phil take me home for a while.

The Proposal

I had only been home two days when I got word from the Palace Movie Theatre that they needed an usherette. I had previously applied so I responded immediately. I started the Friday of that week and didn't tell Phil in my letters. When he came, the surprise was on him as I wasn't home. My mother told him where to find me, and he came to the last show so that he could give me a ride home.

He wanted to know all about my new venture. He could tell I was happy. It must have been that I tried so hard and finally got this job without help from anyone. I would get twelve shillings a week with one night off but no work on Sundays. I started at 1:30 p.m. and worked until 11:00 p.m. with a break from 4:30 p.m. to 6:00 p.m. I also got one free pass each week for a member of my family. I simply loved this job especially when there was a good movie because then we were so busy and the time would fly.

All the girls took their turn in walking up and down the aisles during intermission to sell chocolate bars, cigarettes, and peanuts. I soon made friends with some of the girls, but one of them stood above the rest. Her name was Dorothy Stevenson.

Dot, as she was called, was a nice looking girl with black hair and the prettiest blue eyes with long lashes. I soon found out she had a boy friend whose name was Joe Stenton. I got to meet him one Saturday night when he came to the show.

Joe wasn't very tall, but he certainly was dark and handsome. It so happened he also owned a motor bike with a side car attached. When Phil came the following weekend, he and Joe soon got acquainted. Joe worked at one of the coal mines. He was a mechanical engineer. He was in charge of the cages that took the men up and down the mine. He encouraged Phil to go with him on occasions to the motor cycle races at Donnington Speedway. I was glad they shared something in common. Phil hadn't seen much of his other friends since he left the Danum Bakery.

I was enjoying my sense of security, and Mother was enjoying the privacy of her home again. She was able to take care of Jean for a while before she started school that year. We saw a lot of Betty in her first years because she lived close to us and Mother and Dad grew very fond of her.

These kind of arrangements were much closer to Mother's heart than any horse racing. Toward the end of the year, Phil wrote in his letter that he had a surprise for me so I was eager for his next visit. When he came I could tell he was happy about something, and sure enough, he had finally gotten his degree. That wasn't all, he had also gotten a different job with more pay. The new job was in Mansfield, near Nottingham only 45 miles away. I usually spent Sunday mornings with him, but this Sunday was different. He drove me to Dad's place at Bessacarr. It was very cold so he made a fire and we huddled close to keep warm. Phil was very quiet for a while, then suddenly he said, "Are you ready to marry me?"

I answered, "Well, of course I'm ready to marry you, but are you asking me to marry you right now?"

Then he said, "Well not right this minute, but I have been giving it a lot of thought. We are spending too much time apart and we should give some thought to spending that time together. It has been over four years since I left home and I'm tired of living in lodgings and of all the travelling back and forth. I think we should get a little house we could call our home and stay put for a while."

I told him this made me very happy, and I couldn't wait to get married. However, since he had this new job in Mansfield, it wasn't going to be easy to get a house. There was a great shortage of housing everywhere, and I knew he wouldn't want to live with our parents, as many young couples ended up doing those days, and neither did I. We decided we would get married the following year, but we would wait until after Christmas to set a date.

When I saw Phil take off that day, I waited, as usual, at the door until he got to the top of the street. As I caught the sight of the "Sinutro" flag blowing fiercely in the wind, I waved him good-bye. I came inside and started to cry softly. My mother was concerned until I told her they were happy tears. I suddenly had this wonderful feeling of sheer delight and thought to myself that I was the luckiest girl in the world. Then I told Mother we were finally going to be married.

My thought, at that moment, went all the way back to our first meeting and how I was so worried about the shape of my legs. It was as though Phil never even noticed them, yet, he had to have seen they weren't exactly straight. Maybe it was the same compassion that he showed for his friend Les that allowed him to overlook the obvious in me. Whatever it was, I repeat, I felt extremely lucky and to this day I find it hard to understand how a person who had such a funny sense of humour could also maintain a distinct feeling of compassion.

Phil went to be with his parents for Christmas. We had decided to buy some practical things for each other. We did splurge and went to a New Year's Eve dance. I managed to get off work early so, at least, we were able to get a few hours of dancing and welcome in the year that we would be married, 1937. During the dance, he told me he had broken the news of our impending marriage to his family and, by their reaction, he wasn't sure if they approved or not. This made me feel somewhat uncomfortable. He also said he went to visit his old employer, Mr. Showell. This bakery, in Barton-Under-Needwood, was where he worked on weekends before he left school and after he failed to get into the navy. He started his first full-time job there. Phil was telling Mr. Showell about our situation and he immediately offered him a job, saying that we might have a better chance finding a place to live in a small village rather than in a large town. Phil said he would think about it.

Well, now he was asking me, but I couldn't help him in this matter. I know he had been making all kinds of inquiries about housing in Mansfield, without any results. This was his first real dilemma. We did talk it over and he decided he would stay with this new job for a while.

The Wedding

We made a definite date of Saturday, September 4th, to be married. If by the end of June we hadn't found a place, Phil would take Mr. Showell's offer. I could tell he didn't really like the idea because, for him, it was like taking a step backward.

It was a good thing I had my job to keep me occupied those first few months, otherwise I might have been discouraged. I couldn't really make any plans under these circumstances. Another situation was keeping me busy at the time. My sister Lucie had her third child, Edna. I helped her in the mornings before I went to my work at the cinema.

I knew having the wedding at home was the only way I could expect my parents to attend. It was a miracle that my mother left the house once a year to go downtown just two miles away. It would be the same for Phil's parents because they let us know that anywhere but their home would be out of the question for them to attend.

I also got tired of all the free advise from every source about what I should wear. I wanted to please myself and wear a white bridal gown, but much to my regret, I gave in to peer pressure and did what was considered practical.

Anyway, it didn't make any sense since the wedding was finally planned at Phil's home. I was happy for him. At least we were getting married in St. James Church where he had been a choir boy for eight years.

He came to see me every weekend now but finally the suspense was getting to him so he made the move to work for Mr. Showell. Fortunately, about two weeks later, he heard of a cottage becoming vacant at the end of August, so he applied for it immediately. Philip thought that, for this reason alone, he had done the right thing and I was happy to go along with his decision. He admitted later that, not only was this his first dilemma, but it was also his first big mistake.

One weekend when he came, I went with him to get measured for a suit and the tailor suggested I also have a suit cut from the same cloth for the wedding. We both liked the idea because it was a little different. We went ahead and my measurements were taken at the same time. I know a groom is not supposed to know what his bride is wearing but I really didn't have much choice.

The cloth for the suits was a fine woolen serge in a medium beige color with just a hint of brown thread running through. I found a pretty Crepe de Chine blouse in brown with small flowers of autumn shades. These colors did compliment my suit. To complete the outfit, I bought a fine straw hat in brown. This was a bonnet shape with an upturned brim and small lace veil. I would wear a pair of brown suede pumps with small bows and brown kid leather gloves.

We were both getting anxious about the cottage for the simple reason we would only have a few days in which to do any work on it, if necessary. Due to this concern, I didn't have much time to dwell on the main event except to feel a little sad. I was facing the most important day of my life without any of my family around me. However, our friends Dot and Joe would be there and Dot would be the bridesmaid while Phil's sister Edith would be my maid of honor. These two young ladies wore dresses and hats that were suitable for a small informal wedding.

I worked right up until one week before the wedding, then left my home with my few belongings, including my trousseau and whatever items I had accumulated in my "bottom drawer" (hope chest). A bridal shower was not an English custom at that time so any wedding gifts received were gratefully accepted.

Phil's mother put on a nice luncheon reception for about twenty-five invited guests. My dad paid the expenses and, naturally, Phil made the wedding cake. He had baked the traditional fruit cake months before which had been soaked in brandy and wrapped in cheese cloth. Then the three tiers were covered with almond paste and iced with hard royal icing.

It was truly a masterpiece of architectural design and the style was similar to the exhibition type of wedding cake which Phil had displayed in competition when he was in school. For the top, he was given a beautiful China ornament as a wedding gift from one of the baker's suppliers. They let him have his pick and he chose a very unique one which we always treasured.

We finally got the keys for our home which was called "Myrtle Cottage" and were pleasantly surprised. It was exceptionally clean and just needed a touch of paint here and there. The cottage consisted of two bedrooms upstairs and two front rooms plus a kitchen and bathroom downstairs. There was no hot water but we did have electricity. The two front rooms had little bay windows and small lattice panes of glass. It really looked very charming, very much like a fairy tale cottage. I couldn't wait to move in. Phil's mother was very good in helping with the paint jobs and I was there every day cleaning up any mess. I also had to be there for any deliveries and our furniture.

Our wedding day finally dawned. I hardly slept the night before. I wasn't exactly nervous, I just couldn't contain my excitement. Dot and Joe arrived early, and to my surprise, they brought my little niece, Jean, along with them in their motor bike and side car. At least now I had a member of my family there. The people who owned a grocery store next to Phil's parents, also owned the only taxi in the village. Their wedding gift to us was free taxi service for everyone. As Edith helped me with my corsage of pink carnations, I could tell by her attitude that she approved of her brother's choice.

When we arrived at the church, I was so surprised to see it was full. This made me a little nervous. I hardly knew anyone. As I walked down the aisle holding Joe's arm and saw Phil waiting for me, I got a little lump in my throat. This was the moment I had been waiting for a long time. It was really coming true.

The service didn't take very long, and as we came out of the church, I was even more surprised when I saw all those people waiting to offer their good wishes. Along with Jean, there were two other children that presented us with the traditional good luck, silver horse shoe trimmed with white ribbon and purple heather. I was very touched.

Thanks to Phil's mother, the reception went very well. She was used to arranging such functions, which was another of her many talents. Her arrangements were exceptional.

When it was all over, we said our good-byes to everyone. Our taxi driver then drove us to our new home. Phil soon made a nice fire while I made some tea. We hadn't really had time to inspect every nook and cranny, but as we sat there drinking tea, I suddenly noticed those little bay windows had the prettiest white curtains with the familiar blue willow pattern in small print. I was in love with this place already.

When we went to bed on that first night of our married life, all my pent up emotions and stress of the last few months simply disappeared. As I gave myself to my new husband, who I loved more than life itself, I thought that if this is what they called wedded bliss then it was the most wonderful feeling in the world.

Many years later the famous Harry Belafonte came out with a new song, I think it was called "Nature Boy." The following words from the song were so appropriate for our first night of true love: "The greatest thing you'll ever learn is just to love and be loved in return."

Our First Years

We didn't have a honeymoon; we couldn't afford one, besides the fact that Phil only had his usual Saturday afternoon and Sunday off, which didn't give us enough time. On our first day together, I put my few cooking skills to the test and prepared Phil's favourite dinner of leg of lamb with mint sauce, mashed potatoes and gravy, and fresh garden peas. I did eventually make desserts on occasion, but as I often told Phil, my best desserts came with our marriage license. I was spoiled in that department.

Anyway, on this day, he wanted to make something special, so while I was cooking he was fixing his surprise dessert. He had this planned ahead, so he already had part of it made, and when I saw the finished product it looked so beautiful, it gave me goose bumps. This pastry chef's delight was called a Charlotte Russe. If I'm not mistaken, this is a French version of a glorified English trifle and it tasted every bit as good as it looked. Getting back to dinner, we had just finished eating when my brother, Walter came. He apologized for not attending our wedding. He just couldn't make it, but we were happy to see him, our first visitor.

There was just one problem. We had arranged to go on a charabanc ride (sight-seeing bus tour) that afternoon. Walter agreed to go along with us, even though he had just spent three hours on the train getting here. Anyway, he said it was worth it just to get some of the special dessert.

I was very warmly accepted by the people in the village and soon found ways to occupy my spare time. I went with Phil's mother every Saturday to do the shopping until I got into my own routine. Phil would help his dad with their garden in the afternoon, knowing we would benefit from the fruits of their labor. Saturday night was always reserved for the dance at Barton Hall. On Sundays we would go for a long, pleasant walk, maybe as far as the next village to visit with relatives. The one person I liked best was Phil's little, old Granny Richardson. She was the quaintest little lady I ever saw and reminded me of the painting, "Whistler's Mother" with a shawl around her shoulders. The first time I met her I was surprised to see that she was even shorter than me. She gave me an intense look from her small, sharp eyes as she sized me up. I could tell when she smiled that she approved of me and the feeling was certainly mutual.

Everything went along smoothly for almost a year, but then I could sense that Phil wasn't happy with his job which didn't surprise me. He had no other complaints, but this was his livelihood so it was important. He finally told me he was disappointed at not moving forward as much as he had hoped. His employer seemed to be quite content to go along at his usual pace while Phil was eager to reap the benefit of his experiences. He knew he had made the mistake in returning.

He wrote to Mr. R.C. Hopkinson, one of his former employers of two years at the Danum Bakery in Doncaster and got a reply immediately. Mr. Hopkinson said that he could return to his old job with a better salary. So it was. We left our little cottage and moved back to my home town in late 1938.

We were lucky to find a nice modern house to rent, more expensive of course, and I sadly missed my new friends and the country fresh air. On the plus side, I saw more of my parents and the rest of my family, and we could afford a little more furniture for our bigger house. Phil especially wanted to buy a radio phonograph for our entertainment during the winter months. He bought one, I think it was called "His Masters Voice" put out by R.C.A. He also bought some good records by Montovani, the Dorsey Brothers, Harry James, and others. He enjoyed good music.

Our friends, Dot and Joe Stenton, were married in October of that year so we were able to socialize with them quite a bit. I remember fondly that they did their Christmas merry making on Boxing Day and we were always invited. These were such good times, and they bring back wonderful memories.

The War Years

Early in 1939, Phil and I agreed it would be a good time to start a family and I soon became pregnant with our first child. We were really happy about this. However, our happiness soon became overshadowed by rumors of war. This certainly didn't make for pleasant conversation. Most people were optimistic and eager to dismiss the very thought, but to me it was very scary, especially since I was pregnant.

As the months went by, Hitler was constantly in the news always professing talks of peace. However, he didn't fool anyone except maybe himself. Everyone knew the only peace he wanted was a piece of all the small countries, just as he had already taken a piece of Czechoslovakia. Then he could dominate all of Europe.

When September drew near, we had been warned to expect the worst. Gas masks were distributed to everyone and air raid shelters were being dug underground in all populated areas. On September 1st, when Hitler invaded Poland, we all knew that war was inevitable. Then, on September 3rd, we heard Winston Churchill announce over the radio that since Hitler had not withdrawn his troops from Poland in the given time, we had no choice but to declare war on Germany.

Millions of lives, including ours, would never be the same. That very day, almost every big city turned on the air raid warning for a short period followed by the all clear signal. These tests of the air raid system usually happened in the middle of the night in our city. Even though Phil assured me it was only a test, I was terrified and had an attack of ague. Phil often kidded me because I put on my gas mask preparing for the worst. Who in their right mind wouldn't fear that wailing siren especially during the night.

We had an Anderson type shelter made from some kind of corrugated metal. It was in our back garden and situated half underground and half above ground. It was covered with grass sod, camouflaged to appear like a lawn. We fitted it out with all kinds of emergency items, including food and clothing. There was little or no activity for quite some time, at least not for our country, but other countries were having a bad time.

Our baby wasn't due until mid December, but on November 28, I was sure I was going into labor and Phil got me to the small maternity home only to find it was a false alarm. Because of the war situation, I was advised to stay where I might be safer. Then two days later, on November 30th, our little girl was born at 4:00 a.m. We gave her three names, Heather Dawn Ann. She was tiny, only 4 pounds, 12 ounces, but she was perfect. Because of the rules those days, we had to stay at the maternity home until she weighed 5 pounds.

From then on she made good progress. Heather looked a lot like Phil. She also had big dimples and was a very contented baby. That Christmas we took her to Phil's parents and she was baptized at the church where we were married. Needless to say, there was a lot of fuss over their first grand child, but they were very concerned about her being so small. We never had any cause to worry about her health, but her safety was always my main concern at that time.

My mother, of course, doted on Heather just as she had done with all her grand children and constantly reminded me that she had plenty of time and room to grow. Dad was ruing the fact that with so many girls around, he would eventually not be able to get a word in.

The year 1940, brought a lot of frustration. Young men were being drafted and many were being sent overseas. Ration books were issued, which wasn't too bad at first, but as time passed on food shortages increased. On May 10, the Germans attacked France, and in five weeks they entered Paris. This was a bad day for England and dashed all hopes of the war coming to a sudden end.

Phil was getting restless. The Danum Bakery, like most firms, had cut down on luxury foods and concentrated on mass production of bread to feed the troops. This huge amount of wheat-flour was beginning to have an effect on Phil's sinuses and gave him a bad case of rhinitis (nasal drip). At this point he decided to get away from the situation and thought if he volunteered he could choose the branch of service he wanted rather than wait to be drafted. However, again he failed to pass the physical, so he signed up to work in one of the munitions factories. It was just a matter of waiting for the nearest location.

I am reminded, at this time, of Douglas Bader, a certain Royal Air Force (R.A.F.) pilot who became quite famous. Douglas Bader was already in the service of the R.A.F. prior to the war. He lived with his parents in a small but charming place called Sprotborough, just on the outskirts of Doncaster. His father was a minister of a small church there.

Unfortunately, while performing in a display of aerobatics at Hendon in 1931, his aircraft crashed and the accident resulted in the loss of his legs, one above the knee and the other just below. After being fitted with artificial legs and a considerable time of rehabilitation, he was very unwilling to accept the fact that his career was over. He simply refused to even think that he would never fly again.

Our friend, Joe Stenton, knew Douglas Bader quite well. He had been in the same squadron with him when he was in the R.A.F. reserves. On a trip to England, Joe and I talked bout this famous hero, and I asked him if all that was written about him was true. Joe stated, absolutely, that it was all true. He also said he was quite cocky at times with every right to be. Joe described him as a ruggedly tough individual with handsome features who enjoyed smoking a pipe.

Anyway, Douglas Bader was most influential in training the young, aspiring pilots of the future which was very important at that crucial time. However, this did not satisfy him and after much appealing and perseverance, the air ministry finally agreed to take him back in November 1939. Sometime later he was given permission to fly, and he made such an impression that he was given several promotions. As a squadron leader, he became one of the great heroes of the Battle of Britain.

It was during one of the bombing raids over Germany that his aircraft was shot down, and he was forced to bail out. On the sudden impact with the ground, his artificial legs became separated from his body. He was picked up in a corn field by two German soldiers. They then drove him to a hospital. His reputation as a courageous, legless pilot was well known so the German officers treated him with respect.

He was provided with a new pair of legs, and he insisted on them sending to England for a spare pair. This way his wife would know that, although his aircraft was lost, he was still alive. His wife filled the hollows of the legs with goodies and tobacco for his pipe. After receiving these, Bader got the idea to steal food for the other, less fortunate prisoners of war by filling the legs with the food, often to the point where they were almost too heavy for him to walk.

During the whole course of his captivity, he made three attempts to escape, but without success, and finally his legs were taken away from him. He then reconciled himself to his fate until the Americans freed him when they went into Germany toward the end of the war.

Some rated Squadron Leader Douglas Bader as the best fighter leader and tactician of World War II and one of the best pilots. He was eventually knighted by the Queen of England, and coming from Doncaster, I too thought of him as a true knight in shining armor.

In 1940, almost everyone was familiar with the sound of enemy bombers and I'm sure the fear they caused. Our anti-aircraft gunfire was an everyday occurrence and deafening to the ears, while at the same time, very comforting.

One day, on my way home from town, with Heather in her pram, I was walking alongside the River Don. Fog was rising, which was not unusual. Suddenly, I heard a German aircraft. I was simply terrified. I couldn't move too fast because of the fog, but whenever I saw a break I would run as fast as my legs could carry me.

It was a well known fact that Sheffield, a city about eighteen miles away, would no doubt, be a target because of its large steel industry. I was wondering, could this be the day? What if this pilot was lost in the fog and what if he dropped his bombs right here by mistake? These thoughts were making me extremely nervous.

When I finally made it home, I immediately pushed our table up against the wall beneath the window, as we had been advised to do. Then I took Heather and sat under the table which was supposed to protect us from being hit by flying objects or glass. Our table had two solid sides to it, which was even better. At this angle, it looked like a little cave. Anyway, we stayed there until I heard the all clear. The next day we were informed there was actually no fog. What I had seen was a smoke screen put up by the R.A.F. to divert the German pilot from his target.

From now on, we were to spend many nights in the air raid shelter, but if the activity occurred during the day, I was too scared to make my way to the shelter. Thus, Heather and I spent many, many hours under the table. I was always thankful she was so good, and usually slept most of the time, while I was a nervous wreck. I kept my knitting bag handy. I found that while knitting kept me busy, it also helped to relax my frayed nerves and also provided the much needed sweaters for all of us during the cold winter.

While we were waiting to relocate, Phil stayed with his job at the bakery, and it wasn't long before we had a real close call. Early one morning just after he left the house, there was no warning siren, just a loud explosion. It sounded so close, I was afraid for Phil and his co-workers. Everything in the house shook. It was still dark, so I quickly picked Heather up and made my way to the shelter. This was difficult with such a small ray of light from a pencil flashlight (the margin of light we were allowed in the dark). It was so cold and seemed like hours before the all clear sounded. Then came the waiting to hear if Phil was OK, that was always a time of suspense. We did find out the reason for the explosion on that evening's news broadcast. It seems the local home guards had spotted what they thought was a pilot coming down by parachute. However, this pilot was a dummy with a land mine attached, so that when the guards rushed to it, 14 of them were killed in the explosion and practically the whole street was wiped out. This was just over a mile away and too close for comfort.

In the meantime, Phil's sister Edith became engaged to a young man she had known a long time. His name was Jack Wright, and he lived in the village at Barton-Under-Needwood. Jack was already in the army so they planned to marry when he came home on leave. Edith left her job as a cook and made her home with Jack's parents for the duration of the war. She then went to work in a munitions factory which made Bren guns. This factory was formerly a plant where the German Daimler cars were made but had now been commandeered by the British government. Edith was sure Phil could get a job at this factory. Of course, it would mean moving back there, and we didn't care for the idea, but it would be safer, there were no other large industries close by. However, there was a bomb site which housed an arsenal of bombs for the R.A.F. at Hanbury. We gave some thought to going back in the spring, meanwhile Edith would seek a place for us to live.

During that summer and fall, the German Luftwaffe, under the command of Reich Marshall Hermann Goering began bombing British airfields and forts during the day. Our R.A.F., although they were outnumbered, had better planes and pilots, so they were able to shoot down a larger percentage of the German aircraft, thereby forcing the enemy to switch to night raids. This was when the poor people of London suffered terrible losses, they were bombed out of their homes night after night, losing everything they possessed but worst of all they lost their families. This became known as the London Blitz, but somehow the survivors would manage to emerge from the ruins. The next day, they could be seen dancing in the streets as they sang one of their favourite songs made famous by the British singer Vera Lynn--"There'll be Blue Birds over the White Cliffs of Dover, Tomorrow, when the World is Free," but that tomorrow was so far away.

It only took a few words from Winston Churchill to give new hope to their brave spirits. It was after one of the fiercest air battles during the Battle of Britain that bulldog (Churchill) gave his most famous speech of all--"Never in the field of human conflict, has so much been owed by so many, to so few." This was followed by the his well known statement--"WE WILL NEVAAAH SURRENDAAH."

From then on, great measures were taken to step up the war effort at home as well as on the front line. Many young single women were urged to join the services in some capacity. Everyone was urged to do their patriotic duty, which included planting a vegetable garden (victory garden) to help feed their families. It also became necessary to ration clothing.

Because of the fact we were planning to move as soon as possible, I made sure we spent that Christmas visiting all our relatives, to say good-bye. Aunt Alice and Uncle Fred had not seen much of Heather, and having no children of their own, they got very attached to her. I realized at the time, just how much of her young life had been spent in and out of air raid shelters, which was a far cry from what we had planned for her, from the time she was conceived. Her first birthday came and went without much hoopla, and soon after, she began to walk.

I consoled myself that we were not the only parents with such disappointments. I only had to think about those poor people from London and their terrible ordeal of the London Blitz. We were lucky to be alive, let alone still being together. I especially made a point of seeing my brother, Walter, knowing at anytime he would be drafted into one of the armed forces.

Early in 1941, we packed up our belongings and went back to live in Barton-Under-Needwood, and the air raids continued. It was at this particular time that my dad was able to accomplish his life-long ambition of working in the racing stables.

Since the start of the war, he had always kept busy, but his big chance came when he was asked to help out at the stables of Mr. Smallwood at a place called Swinton. It seemed they were in need of assistance until they could get real experienced stable hands. What started out as a job for a few weeks, turned into almost a year, and due to the kindness of some of the much younger horsemen, Dad learned a lot. He was shown the correct way of strapping and riding, and how to manage a real race horse. Mr. Smallwood said that, had Dad's age of 61 been reversed, he would have had the job there for life. Much to his regret, after twelve months of the happiest time in his life, it was time for him to leave.

From then on he spent a lot of time fire-watching at night, not just at the Danum Bakery, but at a large variety store downtown. He would be perched on the rooftops and this scared my mother, especially after a bomb dropped one night just a couple streets away.

Edith had sent word, before we left Doncaster, that the only thing available for us in Barton was a large storage room, above a small pub (The Red Lyon). Phil had no trouble getting hired at the munitions factory, so we crammed ourselves into this place for the time being. We were lucky, indeed, to have the luxury of a fireplace, a toilet, and a sink, but there was no hot water. In this tiny, living quarters, we were able to set up our bed and Heather's crib and high chair, a small table, and a couple of chairs. I bought a two burner hot plate, and I just did the best I could under the circumstances. The small pub catered mostly to older villagers, so it was fairly quiet, and we were able to sleep well. However, I often took Heather out in her stroller in search of somewhere decent for us to live.

Phil would be working long hours, leaving home at 6:00 a.m. and returning home by 7:00 p.m. He would get Saturday afternoon and the full Sunday off every other week. He also joined the factory's volunteer fire department which was formed to protect the plant from incendiary fire bombs. He was lucky to have a hot meal every day in their canteen. On Sundays, his mother would have us all over for a good, cooked meal so for this we would share our ration coupons.

There's no doubt I did feel safer in Barton, but I also wondered how the people felt about us leaving here three years ago, and now coming back and expecting to find a place to live. I soon found I had no need to worry. One look at Heather was enough. She could melt anyone's heart with her smile and dimples. During my search, I ran into a family of newcomers to the village, Mrs. McNeilly and her six children; three boys and three girls. They had moved from Canada just before the war started. Ettie, as she was called, was from Scotland. Her husband Bob was Irish, and because he was in the regular army, he was sent overseas as soon as the war broke out.

This lady was amazing. She was also very attractive, even though she was prematurely grey which gave her a distinguished look. She had beautiful, big eyes set wide apart, and when she smiled it showed her wonderful personality. With all of this, her Scottish brogue, and the patience of Job, no wonder I liked her the moment I saw her. Ettie turned out to be one of the kindest people I had ever known, and we became very good friends. I think her children, ranging from three to fourteen, kept her young at heart. She was also very much in love with her husband, just as I was with Phil, so I felt very sorry for her being alone and having to raise the children by herself.

She soon let me know that I could leave Heather with her at any time. As she so pleasantly put it, "One more added to my brood would make little difference."

Finally, after almost eight months, I found a small cottage very similar to the one we first lived in. It was directly across the street from St. James church. We were out of that storage room in no time, and I worked hard to get the cottage looking nice and more like a home again for Phil. Although we didn't see very much of him, we spent some happy hours in the comfort of that little cottage.

December 7, 1941 came and so did Pearl Harbor. America was brought into the war, and as 1942 arrived, I'm sure I was in the majority in wondering what was going to happen now. It was a horrible year of turmoil and uncertainty. Would there ever be an end to all the fighting and bombing? Black marketing and profiteering were on the rampage, and it seemed as though patriotism was beginning to lose some of its grip. Those who were holding down the fort, on the home front, seemed to be stretched to the limit of their endurance.

In the spring of 1943, Heather was now three so I decided to do some volunteer work where I could include her, or leave her with Mrs. McNeilly if need be. By a mere coincidence, one day I ran into Mrs. Robinson in the village. This was the lady I had worked for in service back in 1936. I knew that people of her status with large estates were not allowed to keep more than one maid at this time of war. I also knew that Mrs. Robinson was very much involved with the Red Cross, and that she had taken two young boys into her home. They were evacuees from Birmingham who came for safety. Anyway, she gently addressed me, as she always did, by saying, "My dear child, would you be interested in helping me for a few hours a day?" Knowing she was doing her part to help the war effort, I agreed to give it a try, and as I glanced toward Heather, she quickly added, "Do bring your little girl with you. I'm sure we'll get along very well."

And so it was, I went back to the Dower House as a part time maid. Mrs. Robinson's daughter, Miss Mavis, was now a nurse, so we didn't see very much of her. However, Mrs. Ames was still working on Fridays, and the little old gardener was still there.

I limited my time from 9:00 a.m. to 3:00 p.m. with time out for lunch. I just did whatever I could and hoped it would be enough. It must have been satisfactory, I stayed for just over a year, and Heather got along with Charlie Apted (the young boy from Birmingham) just fine. His brother went back home. I think he was homesick.

I wonder, to this day, where Charley might be. Mrs. Robinson told me that at one time she had considered letting him stay after the war, and train him to be a butler. I know she would have been good to him.

During that year, the Robinsons took a two week vacation and asked if Phil and I would stay at the estate in their absence and take care of everything, including Charlie. I felt somewhat honored to be trusted with such a responsibility, which turned out to be a pleasant experience because it took our minds off the war for two weeks. I could hear my dad saying, "You're getting up in the world, Genty." I might add, we also got paid very well.

As we proceeded into the year 1944, there was a certain feeling everywhere which told us that something big was going to happen. I had the feeling that we could all breathe a little easier because more and more Americans were coming to our aide, in spite of the fact they were also dealing with war in the Pacific. It wasn't long before our suspicions were confirmed. We were made aware that plans for the D-Day invasion of France were being made. We were never told when or where the landing would take place. This was a time of excitement on one hand and anxiety with fear on the other. There was never any doubt that the Allied forces would be victorious. However, little did we realize, until after the invasion was over, how the horror and tremendous death and destruction would change the whole world and how our success was so painfully achieved.

After France was liberated, the big question on everyone's mind was, "Has it been worth the enormous loss of lives?" The answer was clear. Had not all those brave men made the final, ultimate sacrifice for their country, the murderous Adolf Hitler would have been victorious.

Consequently, we would all have been living under the rule of the Third Reich and Facism.

A lot of families were expecting their heroes home for the Christmas of 1944 but the war was still far from over. Phil and I started going to the Saturday night dances at Barton Hall and we took Heather along with us. The band had been reduced to one person playing the piano. There were no real musicians available, at least not for a small, country village.

One week-end, Phil got the idea to take our phonograph to the hall and play the records. We had just bought some new ones by the great Glen Miller, who was popular at that time. This was such a hit with the young crowd that we were asked to do it on a regular basis, and when Phil had to work, I did it alone. We were given two new records every week, so together with our own, we had a good selection. All the proceeds from the dances went to the Red Cross fund, so that gave us a certain satisfaction, and I could now call myself a disc jockey. Also, we were encouraging the many teenagers to spend Saturday nights dancing, instead of being drawn to the pubs to drink.

Unfortunately, that year we experienced a very sad incident. It happened one Sunday when Phil was home. It was about 11:00 a.m. and suddenly we heard a terrible explosion. It was almost like an earthquake, things began to shake and rattle. Phil and his mother sensed what it was immediately--"The bomb site at Hanbury." They both got on their bicycles and headed for the small village, with one fearful thought in mind. Her 84 year old mother lived at Hanbury by the side of the church. They didn't get very far when they were stopped by the military and told they would be notified as soon as possible. That same evening they got word that Grandmother Page was safe, and except for a few shattered windows, the small church was intact but the worst was yet to come.

There was a marble pit not far from the bomb site and most of the men in the surrounding villages worked in this pit. We were informed the next day that it received the full blast of the explosion and that forty-four men were killed including five of Phil's, mother's relatives. There were two of her brothers, one brother-in-law, and two nephews. Also, where there had been a field and a farmer operating a tractor, there was now a huge crater and no sign of the farmer or his tractor. This was indeed a very sad day.

We were never told exactly what happened, but the general consensus was sabotage. It was a common sight to see prisoners of war strolling the country roads in pairs. Although they appeared harmless, it just didn't seem right that they should have the privilege. With these circumstances, anything was possible.

Although the war was not yet over, Phil was concerned about his baking. He hadn't worked at his real trade for over four years. He wondered how long it would take for rationing to cease before we would be able to start afresh, and he was mulling over what his next course of action would be. I understood his concern. Many times in the past, he had talked about emigrating, but I never took him seriously. When he brought it up again, I began to wonder. Did he really have something in mind?

As the war years passed, Heather was growing up. Her 5th birthday was coming up soon, then Christmas would be upon us and I wanted to do something special for her. So far there had been little to celebrate, but we did have many reasons to thank God. We bought a small Christmas tree, but it was impossible to buy the usual kind of tree ornaments, so I put my resources to work, and came up with an idea.

Over the years when the British used radar (a carefully guarded secret development) to track attacking planes, they would also drop tiny strips of metal foil from their aircraft to confuse the enemy radar. After the raids, the streets were littered with roll ends of this metal foil, or chaff, which looked like silver ribbon. The kids, including Heather, were always on the lookout for this war souvenir, which came down from the sky. So I turned that silver ribbon into stars, bells and icicles, and everything else imaginable to put on the tree. Together, with tiny bows of red and green yarn, we had a real festive looking tree. Holly always grows in such profusion in England so I used that to trim around the house and the fireplace, which complimented the tree. Heather was delighted with the results so it made all my efforts worthwhile.

That same Christmas we got a nice army type greeting card from my brother, Walter. He was serving with General Alexander's army. I think they were in Italy at that time so I continued to pray for his safe return home. Just a few days after Christmas, one of the small villages close by was invaded by a large number of American G-I's for the sole purpose of knocking the stuffing out of Adolph Hitler, as they so aptly put it. It was also the time, as I recall, that Glen Miller was reported missing on his way over from the United States to entertain the troops. This was a sad blow for lovers of good music everywhere, he would be greatly missed.

We had a gala event that New Year's Eve. We had managed to obtain a live band, so Phil and I were looking forward to this, our first New Year's Eve dance since the war began. Phil's mother was going, too, and we encouraged Mrs. McNeilly to go with her pretty (now teenage) girls. She usually stayed home with the boys, but I thought this would be fun for her. Besides, who better to sing Auld Lang Syne with and to wish--"Lang Mae Yer Lum Reek" to, than a true Scot.

The evening was a huge success, the young people literally had a ball. The band started off by paying a tribute to Glen Miller, and continued playing his music for most of the dances. Word got around about this live band, so much to the delight of all the young girls it wasn't long before quite a few Americans showed up. I don't think I ever hear, "In the Mood," "Boogie Woogie Bugle Boy," and "American Patrol" without thinking of that night. Those GI's really knew how to jive and jitterbug. They even showed Heather how to do it. They paid a lot of attention to her, and I'm sure it was because most of them had little children back home.

When we left, Phil invited a few of the GI's to our home so they could listen to the New Year greeting still being broadcast from their homes. This was all right by me, but I was concerned about what I would give these men to eat. They all looked as if they had the appetite of a horse and my cupboard was quite bare. The only thing I had, besides plenty of bread, was a can of red salmon so I simply mashed this with a fork and managed to stretch it into several sandwiches. I also had a fruitcake, saved from Christmas, and sliced it very thin. They carried coffee with them. Apparently they weren't thrilled with our tea. This seemed so little to offer, but maybe the thought of befriending them, rather than what we had to offer, was enough for them to thank us and to assure us they would come to the dance the following week.

We continued to play records at the dances, and when the Americans found that Phil was a baker, they invited him to their camp to bake for them on his day off. They also had a hospital set up for the wounded from the 101st Airborne Division, and they got Phil to make special cakes for these wounded. They were short of nothing for baking, so this was a treat for Phil. They had five men in charge of their cooking, and each one was a different nationality. This really made an impression on Phil. He told me many times that because they got along so well, America must be a good place to live.

Everyone was curious to know when they were leaving, but they weren't allowed to say. One day they just wouldn't show up. At that time, we would know they were on their way to Germany. They bragged about everything being over when they got there, which was true. It didn't take long before the war came to an end, "V-Day" on May 8, 1945.

Phil received a nice letter, written on paper that was bordered with flags of the United Nations. This was sent from the hospital and signed from the boys in Ward 18. Later on, we got another letter and a menu for their last Christmas dinner on Uncle Sam. This was from the Battery Personnel in Battery C., 564th Field Artillery Battalion, number 71, somewhere in

Germany. We often wondered how many of them made it home, and if they ever realized their influences had persuaded Phil to immigrate to the United States.

Phil continued working at the factory right up to the end of the war in the Pacific, "VJ-Day" in August, 1945. At the end of the war came rejoicing and celebrating. Every street had their own huge party. It seemed to go on for days. It was truly the most wonderful feeling. We could now sleep at night in our own beds without any fear. I'm glad my brother came home safe. Shortly after, he got married, got his old job back, and started a new life.

Emmigration

After all the excitement diminished, Phil became very serious about leaving England and explained to me the reasons why. He felt that he would not be able to do the specialty baking work he had been trained to do because of rationing, product shortages, and other war-related restrictions in England. He also did not know how long this situation would last and he did not want to wait. He was hoping I felt the same way, but if not, he would wait for a while and discuss the subject later. I didn't understand some of his reasons, but my mind was already made up. I would go anywhere with him, if that's what he wanted. The last six years of fear and frustration had not exactly been the most romantic, but our love was still as strong as ever. We started planning by making sure we could work for Uncle Fred in the market and stay with my parents. We sold most of our possessions and went back to Doncaster in September 1945. Then we started the procedure of immigrating and were told that war brides were given first priority.

We soon learned we were about to be strangled by the red tape of immigration laws. We didn't have a sponsor, and we weren't financially strong enough to enter the country on our own. When Phil drove south to buy produce for the market, he often took time to check with the American Consul in London to see if the situation was improving, but they never gave him any encouragement, or hope, for that matter.

After about a year, my mother's sister who lived in Canada had written to suggest we go to "God's Country," Canada, instead. Finally, out of desperation, we decided if we went there, we might have a better chance of getting into the United States. This made it easier for us because we didn't need a sponsor to enter Canada. My aunt just had to declare she would be responsible for us until we got established. Of course we did have to wait for a boat. War brides also got first priority to Canada.

In the meantime, Phil invested our money in a big, 1936 American Chrysler that, supposedly, had a taxi license with it. The price of this car was the equivalent of 5,000 dollars, and we only had half that amount to put down, so we would pay the remainder in monthly payments.

Phil soon got plenty of jobs taking families to seaside resorts on Sundays. Then he brought them home the following week. Together, with his work for Uncle Fred, he was working long hours, but he was making good money.

We had made up our minds to emmigrate. Heather had already done some schooling in Barton-Under-Needwood and was going to school in Doncaster. When there was no school, she spent time with Aunt Alice and Uncle Fred. This was always fun time, and they were getting closer to her. I know it was going to be hard for them when we left. My dad even suggested we leave Heather with them until we got established in Canada, but we could never leave without her.

Every morning when my dad read his paper, he would be quick to point out anything that would discredit America. This was one of his ways of letting me know he didn't approve of our move, and as time went on, we had many disagreements. He would also bring up the subject of racism and did I know that they have six months of winter. He hoped to discourage me, but I usually came up with an appropriate answer.

One day he asked, "What will you do if Phil gets sick?"

I said, "Well then, I would go to work for him."

I will never forget what he said next, "I'll tell you this much Genty, if every woman stood behind her man the way you stand behind yours, this world would be a lot better place to live in."

I knew, at that moment, he was not angry with me, only sad at the thought of us leaving and he wasn't about to let go of his Genty without a fight.

Early in 1947, we got the worst snow storm of our life time. Many people died during that terrible winter, including Phil's dad. We received a telegram one day telling us the news of his unexpected death. He was only 56 years old. It was treacherous driving, but Phil and I went to Barton-Under-Needwood to be with his mother. The funeral was delayed several days because the burial site was frozen solid. Apparently, his dad was very sick with bronchial pneumonia, and he was too weak to fight the disease.

Because we were still getting strong blizzards, it was at least three weeks before it was safe to drive back to Doncaster. Just after we got home, we were offered a passage to Canada on one of the Cunard White Star Liners, but we didn't have the heart to leave Phil's mother at that time. However, we thought it would be a good idea to start packing some things in case we got another offer. We also had to think about selling the car to get our investment money back.

During the next few months, we managed a little respite here and there. We even talked my mother into taking a trip to a coastal town but we had to practically twist her arm.

Just before our tenth anniversary drew near, we were dealt a cruel blow. It was broadcast on the B.B.C. one night that there would be no more petrol (gas) for the private motorist until further notice. I cringed at this news, but Phil said we were OK because we had the taxi license. However, nothing was further from the truth. Each time Phil made a payment on the car, the dealer would tell him he had forgotten to transfer the license, but now, much too late, he told us he didn't know the license was not transferable. Also, much too late, we realized this car dealer was something I choose not to put in print.

Ironically, about mid-September, we had another offer of passage to Canada, departing on November 7th. I just couldn't believe that this could happen to us, and I felt so sorry for Phil. He didn't know what to do. All our money to pay for the passage, plus train fare across Canada, was tied up in the car. We did have some cash, but nowhere near enough. No sane person would buy that big car if they couldn't get the petrol to run it. It would be like trying to sell coal to Newcastle or snow to an Eskimo. So the question was, should we wait (who knows how long) until we were able to buy the petrol again or should we sell whatever we had left and take that boat on November 7th? We took some time to ponder over our dismal situation before we made the decision to take the risk.

To start with, the dealer wanted nothing more to do with the car. He was only interested in getting the remainder of his money, which by now wasn't all that much. Anyway, with the help of a few of our friends, we pressured the dealer into a settlement. He offered to wipe out the balance that we owed, then gave us a small car (a Sunbeam Talbot), and we gave him back the Chrysler. This was a rotten deal, but when you deal with a shark you usually get bitten.

We didn't really have much choice at this point so we took the Sunbeam Talbot and even that was hard to sell, but we pitched in and decided to have a sale. We were determined not to let this get us down. Everything I had considered essential to take with us had to be sold, plus quite a few treasures. Because clothing was still rationed, Phil sold two good suits and his gold watch. People were glad to buy clothing but mine wasn't so easy to sell because of my small size. However, I did own a good astrakhan fur coat. Phil didn't want me to part with it. He thought I needed it for the cold Canadian winter, but we needed the money more, so I let it go.

One day while I was downtown, I went to see Mr. Thompson, the jeweler. Phil had bought my engagement ring from him over twelve years ago. I explained our situation and asked him how much money I could get by pawning the ring. To my surprise, he offered me exactly ten times as much as Phil had originally paid for it. I told Mr. Thompson I would only do this if he would save the ring, and I would send the money for interest until I could afford to redeem it once again.

I was definitely out of Phil's favour for a while, but I told him, "At least, now, we have enough money to pay our fares plus a little to spare."

My mother had given me her trunk which she used when she went into domestic service but all that we had left to put in it was a few everyday clothes, two woolen blankets, and a hand-carved, oak-framed mirror which my dad had made at the Leeds School of Art.

Early on the morning of November 7th, we said good-bye to most of my family except my dad. He left the house at the crack of dawn and didn't return until we had gone. The hardest thing was saying good-bye to my mother. As far as she was concerned, Phil could do no wrong so she was happy for us. It was also hard leaving our good friends, Dot and Joe. By this time they had three children, a girl and two boys. They drove us to the train station and gave us a happy send-off. We traveled to London. From there we got the boat train to Southhampton.

We were both really exhausted, but when we got on that last train we gave a big sigh of relief and Phil did his best to convince Heather and me that, from now on, everything was going to be OK.

Heather was very excited about the big boat, and Phil kept telling me this was going to be our delayed honeymoon cruise, but that turned into a big joke. The minute we stepped onto the "Aquitania," which was still on austerity travel, the directions were right there, as large as life: "Women and children to the right and men to the left." We weren't even allowed to sleep together. I can laugh about it now, but it wasn't funny at the time.

I had been romantically fantasizing about that first night aboard ship. We had been so preoccupied by all the problems and wondering if we were really going to get away that we didn't take the time to fill our own emotional needs. Then, just when we thought we had the perfect opportunity for a night of long-overdue love making, we were denied. I think that was the first time I cried throughout this ordeal. We were only allowed to eat meals together and roam around on the top deck but the crossing was very blustery and wet. I'm sure that Phil was just as disappointed as I was.

Before we slipped away into the dark night from Southampton, we were served our first meal. This was a real treat. The pure white bread, alone, was a gourmet delight in comparison to the grey looking bread we had been eating for the past few years. The rest of the food was delicious, and by and large, the voyage itself was most enjoyable. Pity we couldn't say the same for the sleeping arrangements.

We landed in Halifax, Nova Scotia, and got straight onto a waiting train to take us to British Columbia. Our first stop was for several hours at Winnepeg, Manitoba, where most of the travelers took advantage to shop, in spite of the blizzard-like weather. The night before we left home, my dad had given Heather a five pound note to spend when she touched Canadian soil and we had about fifty dollars. The first thing we did was buy food. We had brought surplus food from the boat, such as fruit and cookies, but this five day train journey was going to take more than that to feed us. It was so good to be able to buy as much as we wanted without coupons. Heather was able to get a good, warm parka with Eskimo fur around the hood and a pair of snow boots with her money. She insisted on wearing them right there in the store.

Once we got back on the train, we tried to get some sleep which was difficult. We had to make do with pillows and blankets as this was no luxury travel. We made several shorter stops but the further we traveled, the less harsh the weather became. Finally on November 17th, we came to the end of the line, which was a small place called Castlegar. My Aunt Jessie and Uncle Cliff (Brandt) were there to meet us and drove us the rest of the way to their home in Trail, B.C., about 15 miles further.

Canada/Trail, B.C.

Trail was a small, friendly town in British Columbia, which reached across both sides of the Columbia River. The main work force there was the Consolidated Mining and Smelting Company (COMINCO) of Canada. Uncle Cliff was employed here as a boss on the labor gang.

Although we were warmly received, I felt somewhat of a stranger. I could only remember my aunt from pictures. She had left England at a young age to work in service on a farm in Saskatchewan. She was very petite at about 5 feet 2 inches. She bore no resemblance to my mother but this was mostly because she dressed very fashionably. Uncle Cliff was a big man, about 6 feet tall. He was very soft spoken and extremely polite. Financially, they appeared to be comfortably well off, they had no children.

We all needed sleep badly because we got very little on the train, but the very next day Auntie Jessie had plans for us. She took us down to meet Joe Merlo, an Italian who owned and operated the City Bakery. He hired Phil on a Friday, and he began working on Monday.

Phil was so relieved, we were down to our last few dollars so he was anxious to get started. He was a little apprehensive at first, knowing he hadn't been inside a bakery for almost five years. However, when he came home that first day, he was all smiles. Joe had told him to just feel his way around until he knew where he would fit in comfortably.

Luckily he made a hit right away. It seems Joe had purchased a large cookie machine about six months previously and it just sat there. No one knew how to operate it. Phil got it started right away and proceeded to turn out loads of cookies, while at the same time, showing the others how it was done. Phil also told me he had met Joe's wife, Irma, and their three young sons, his brother Alphonso, and several other relatives. They all worked in the bakery and lived in the apartments directly above. Irma did all of the cooking. The young ladies who worked in the store spoke English, but they also spoke fluent Italian so it didn't take long for Phil to pick up the language, especially the swear words. It was easy to see that Phil was happy to be back in his own trade again. He was getting his sense of humour back which was a good sign.

For the first few months we were able to save a little money so I sent a food package to both our parents. They weren't starving by any means but food was still rationed while we had the choice of everything and we were anxious to share it. As I had promised, I also sent to the jewelers the money to pay the interest on my ring.

In the meantime, my aunt had given a welcoming party for us which was more like a bridal shower, and we received many of the essentials which we needed to get back into keeping house once more.

After Christmas we started looking for a place to rent, and I got a job as a dish washer in a restaurant. Heather was already enrolled in school, and on her way home she would stop at the restaurant and help me finish up so I could get home and prepare supper.

It wasn't long before Joe Merlo offered to buy a little house for us. He put out the money and deducted the payments from Phil's paycheck. This house was like a palace to us. It was our very own.

I got the best surprise for my birthday that January 1948. It was slightly belated because of the distance in transit. Although I had told my mother not to send any gifts because the postage was so expensive, I still received a package from her. I waited until Phil came home before I opened it, and I found a good supply of yarn and I remarked that at least she sent something practical for my favourite pastime. Upon further inspection, I discovered a small vial of a particular type of aspirin. She probably thought we couldn't get them in

Canada but aspirin wasn't the only thing in that vial. As soon as I picked it out of the yarn, I saw something shining. It was my little engagement ring. I could hardly believe it and I cried tears of joy. I hadn't told my mother about having to pawn it, but I guess my sisters let the cat out of the bag.

A short time later, I got a heartwarming letter from my dad. I was back in his good graces again, and I realized, then, why he didn't come home that day until we had gone. He just couldn't bring himself to say good-bye.

Joe Merlo continued to treat us like we were his family. We were invited to their family picnics, and they got us interested in the Canadian sport of ice hockey which we had never seen before. We soon became avid fans and couldn't wait from one week to the next to see a game. This was amateur hockey played by the "Trail Smoke Eaters" where we saw much more good play than all the fighting seen on the ice in professional hockey today. Heather soon learned to skate which was almost a way of life for children in Canada.

My mother's brother, Edmund, also went to live in Canada and worked at the same farm as Auntie Jessie in Saskatchewan. However, after serving with the Canadian Army in World War I, he and his wife, Marion Victoria, left the prairie and moved west to Vancouver, B.C. The two of them worked very hard raising turkeys. I found this information through different sources, and when I finally located them, Joe Merlo lent us a car so that Phil could drive us to see my long lost relative. As soon as I met Auntie Marion, it was easy to tell she was British to the bone. The walls of their stately home were covered with pictures of all members of the Royal family, and she herself was a look alike for Queen Victoria, or her namesake.

This turned into a wonderful trip. The scenery was spectacular and I loved Vancouver. It was quite a metropolis, even all those years ago. It really fascinated me and seeing English Bay right on the edge of the ocean reminded me of home. We were to become regular visitors to Vancouver. I immediately felt very close to this Aunt and Uncle. They only had one child, a girl, and she died at an early age from whooping cough, so we were looked upon as their kids.

It didn't take long to realize that Auntie Marion was obsessed about making a will, and she eventually told us the reason. It appears her grandfather and two other gentlemen set out from Huddersfield, England, with the intention of making a life for themselves in Western Canada. They did just that but lost their fortune to the legal system because they did not make a proper will.

I wrote to the public library in Vancouver, B.C. and received information which came from the book, "The Vancouver Book," edited by Chuck Davis. The following account from the book tells the story of three men, Samuel Brighouse, John Morton and William Hailstone who came from England in 1862:

> In that same year those characters, now part of Vancouver folklore, bought District Lot 185 for $550.75. Their 540 acres comprised what is now, in its entirety, the West End of Vancouver.
>
> The three of them earned their nickname, *The Three Greenhorns*, for what was considered a frivolous investment in that remote piece of rainforest. They hoped to establish a brick works and build a log cabin on a bluff where today 1053 West Hastings is located. They began farming and even tried to make bricks, but milk and bricks need to be sold, and New Westminster was miles away.
>
> So these men, Vancouver's first white settlers, tried to maintain themselves by finding other work. With Vancouver (still called Granville) growing and hints of the Canadian

> Pacific Railroad (C.P.R.) heading for the Pacific, the "brick makers" offered lots for sale.
>
> Hardly anyone bought lots so in 1886 the three men donated one third of their property to the C.P.R. to attract the railroad to Coal Harbor. They were hoping this would bring people and that people would buy their lots.
>
> In the spring of 1887, the local paper announced the impending sale of acre lots in District Lot 185 for $350.00 to $1000.00 each. Those people who knew something of the C.P.R.'s plans also knew that Stanley Park had just been established at the western end of the peninsula. The C.P.R. Hotel was to be built on the height of land adjacent to District Lot 185, and the C.P.R. planned to cut roads on their property, which bordered the entire length of D.L. 185.
>
> The first permanent settlers of the West End were C.P.R. officials themselves. By 1888 Georgia Street had become a fashionable address, soon to earn the gently derisive sobriquet, "Blueblood Alley." Another finger of respectability, Robson Street, probed the wilderness parallel to it. The name West End first appeared officially in 1887.

So now I can understand my Aunt Marion's frustration when she realized that her grandfather, Samuel Brighouse, didn't make a will for what must have been quite a fortune. Consequently, the millions of dollars he had made was eaten up by attorney fees in traveling back and forth to England trying to locate the rightful heirs. She was one of them, but she never received a penny.

I would like to think in a round-about way that I am a shirt-tail relative (by marriage) to one of the three founders of the West End in the beautiful city of Vancouver, British Columbia, Canada.

We continued to see more of beautiful British Columbia. There were many smaller towns within a short distance of Trail, but the one that struck me most was Rossland. This was a true winter wonderland for skiers and a much higher elevation than Trail. My first sight of this mountainous area of scenic beauty was in sharp contrast to the view we observed as we drove down the constant winding road. When we finally reached the bottom, it seemed like we were going into a huge hollow and barely visible was the city of Trail wrapped in clouds of different shades of smog and smoke which poured from the large chimney stacks of the smelter. We didn't realize at the time just how much effect these fumes had on most of the population. Many workers ended up with lead poisoning and it was difficult to grow any kind of gardens. However, many years later, just like many other big companies, COMINCO made great strides in getting rid of toxic waste and conditions became bearable.

USA/Spokane

Early in 1950, Joe Merlo contacted a wholesale bakery in Spokane, which was 135 miles south of the Canadian border in the State of Washington. He then made an agreement to send Phil there to obtain information on commercial bread baking and in return Phil could pass on his expertise of cake baking.

As I recall, Phil spent two weeks in Spokane and during that time he was invited to a Bakery Engineer's meeting at the Spokane Hotel. That same evening he was asked to give a talk on English baked goods.

Before returning to Trail, he was again invited to the next monthly Engineer's meeting and to give a demonstration of French pastries, petits-fours, etc., so he agreed to go. This turned out to be a turning point in our lives. One man in particular offered to let Phil use his bakery to make the pastries for the demonstration and apparently he was impressed by Phil's work. He immediately asked, "What will it take to persuade you to work for mc."

Phil replied, "I would need a sponsor to get into the United States."

The bakery owner quickly responded with, "You've got one right here."

Phil was taken off guard at first, but then realized the man was really serious and told him, "I will think about it."

When Phil came back to Trail this time, I could tell something was bothering him, and after he explained the situation to me, I understood perfectly how he felt. We had moved to Canada with the sole purpose of trying to get into the United States but now that the opportunity had presented itself, Phil was faced with a terrible dilemma. We were getting along so well and I felt good about earning a little money to help us get on our feet. Phil had said many times that these three years in Canada had been the happiest years of his life.

How could he possibly leave Joe Merlo? He had been kindness itself to all of us. I told him this was one time he would have to make his own decision, but no matter how difficult it was and whatever he decided to do, I would stand behind him all the way.

I think that was the hardest thing Phil ever had to do, but when he talked it over with Joe, he was somewhat relieved. Being the sort of man that Joe was, he didn't seem at all surprised. In fact, he said he knew this had been Phil's ambition, and he wouldn't stand in his way. Joe also made it clear that if things didn't turn out the way we hoped, there would always be a job for him at the City Bakery.

On the day we left, they all wished us well, and Joe gave Phil a gold wrist watch. So, just three years after we had arrived in Canada, we moved to the United States. Once again we started over, only this time we were much better off. We had sold our little house and made a profit of five hundred dollars, which was a small fortune to us (thanks to Joe).

While in Canada we were befriended by a family that came from Stornaway on the northern tip of Scotland, and just like Mrs. McNeilly, they were the salt of the earth. Bill McLeod and his wife Chrissie, his brother Murdo (a confirmed bachelor who lived with them), and their daughter, Norma, who was born in Trail and was Heather's age, made up the family.

Bill and Murdo had worked at the smelter for years and made a good living. Their ancestors were from a long line of McLeods and many of them were hardy sea faring men. They were well known as captains of the boats that made runs on the many lochs in Scotland, as well as on the lakes around Canada.

The old adage that the Scotsman is very frugal and thrifty really belies the true spirit of this particular family. Their generosity, not only to us but to everyone whose lives they touched, was overflowing. I felt very fortunate to have known them, and very sad when we parted.

We entered the United States in October 1950, and went to live in Spokane, Washington. One of the first things we did was to sign a document of intention to become American citizens, at which time we had to wait five years. I was beginning to wonder how Heather felt about being uprooted so many times. It was always a big responsibility for us, but it didn't seem to have any effect on her, or if it did, she didn't show it. She was now eleven years old and had been through many ordeals. We were so proud of the way she behaved and of her good school reports. She was about to enter a new school.

Phil and I both felt a sort of guilt that we hadn't had another child when Heather was younger. I did have a miscarriage in 1942, and then, for obvious reasons, we decided to wait until the war was over. Of course, we weren't to know just how long the war would last, and then during the trials of immigrating we kept putting it off, much to our regret.

Anyway, I got pregnant in 1951, but again I had a miscarriage, and we were afraid we had left it too late. We didn't give up though, and sure enough, in 1952 I carried a pregnancy through and our second little girl was born on December 1, the day after Heather's 13th birthday. We named her Cathy Joanne. She was almost Heather's double. She looked so much like her, dimples and all.

When we first arrived in Spokane, we lived with the couple who sponsored us, Mr. and Mrs. Francis Edmunds and their three children. They owned and operated a good retail bakery business. They also owned a large home with two apartments above it, and we were offered the chance to stay in one of them for a small fee until we found something suitable. We stayed there for two years which gave us a chance to save some money toward a new car.

I'll never forget that car; a '52 Oldsmobile Ninety-Eight. Phil was as happy as a dog with two tails and spent all his spare time cleaning and polishing it. I have to laugh every time I think of when I was pregnant with Cathy and Phil said, "If it's raining when it's time to go to the hospital, you'll be out of luck. You'll have to take a taxi."

We took frequent trips north to Trail, B.C., but just before we got there we would always find a stream and stop to clean the whitewall tires. Our first stop would be the City Bakery and then on to visit the McLeods.

By the time Cathy was a year old, we had moved into a nice home on the Northwest side of town, and there we made many new friends. Heather was now in high school and soon found a job baby sitting right next door to us with the Oman family.

Mr. and Mrs. Trump (Willie and Nina), whom we actually met the first day we arrived in Spokane, also lived in this area and they helped in every way possible to make us feel welcome. They had a beautiful garden and we tried to learn from their experience, but Willie often told the tale of when I dug a trench a foot deep to put in some strawberry plants, that's how much I knew about gardening. We have always remained good friends at all times.

Here I have to mention one more special friend, Thelma Distler. Thelma was a registered nurse and worked in the office of Doctors Petersen and Babcock, who were our family doctors. One day when I took Cathy for her baby shots, Thelma told me she was in need of a baby sitter for her little girl, Diane, and wondered if I was interested in the job. I was a little hesitant at first, but then, I thought I could certainly use a little extra money since we were now buying a home.

It didn't take long for me to realize that it was one of the smartest things I ever did, and I had made another life-long friend. I took care of Diane until she was five years old, at which time Thelma was pregnant with her second child.

The word soon got around about my baby sitting and it wasn't long before I took in a little boy whose name was Gerry. He was about Cathy's age. Gerry lived with his grandmother,

Mrs. Speller. She was a very kind- hearted, elderly lady and very hard working. Because she had a job, I was only too happy to help her out.

I really enjoyed this period in my life with these three little children. They got along very well together. We had a nice yard for them to play in, and with Heather's help, we planned birthday parties and had fun. I also made a lasting impression on them when I gave them my famous banana sandwiches. This was the kind of experience I had missed out on with Heather as a child, and, now here she was, like a second mother to Cathy.

At this time in Cathy's life I couldn't wait to buy her pretty shoes. It was almost an obsession. I think this went back to the time when I couldn't wear shoes until I was fourteen, and I vowed I would make up for it one day. This was something else I couldn't do for Heather. During the war everything was so austere. There was very little choice in shoes or clothing, and most of the time her things were bought from an exchange store. We would trade items of hers that she had grown out of for something larger and for which we paid a small fee.

In the meantime, Phil had been working for Mr. Edmunds, but it wasn't too long before he sold his bakery. Shortly thereafter, Phil was approached by the owner of another good retail bakery which was located in downtown Spokane. Apparently this man had heard of Phil's reputation and offered him a job. Finally, we all seemed to be enjoying some kind of stability. Spokane was, and still is, a very clean and friendly city, and five years exactly from the time we arrived we became American citizens.

Back Home/England

Going back a few years, my sister Elsie obtained a divorce from her husband just after the war ended and after a while, she married a man named Tom Luker. Elsie seemed much happier the second time around. She and Tom had a baby girl and named her Pauline.

By this time, Dad had persuaded Mother to leave the old house in Hyde Park and move into a much larger one, closer to town. When he wrote, he described this house as a mansion, which had all the modern conveniences. Because of all of the rooms in this so called mansion, Elsie and all her family moved in with Mother and Dad.

This seemed to give Mother a new lease on life, and from what Dad wrote, she was running around like a two year old. She was always first in line to watch for the post man because any letter from the United States could not be bought with gold. This made me feel good, but also guilty at times. Maybe I should have written more often.

Because of Dad's gardening experience, he was able to make quite a show place of his town residence, as opposed to his country seat at Bessacarr, where he admitted he took first prize for the best weeds. I heard all about the lawn and his rock garden and how he had built a grotto, some small statues, an archway, and some trellis work. Then he planted the rose bushes and honeysuckle for climbing. In the letter he asked me to take a bow for him. The town councillor had been to take pictures of his handy work to present them at the next council meeting in recognition of his efforts to improve the look of his neighborhood.

From the time I received the first letter from my dad, we kept up a steady correspondence until the time of his death. He wrote a few pages every Saturday night when he was on his job as watchman at the Danum Bakery. He waited a few weeks and then sent them all together. It was almost like having a visit with him.

Once in a while I would bring the letters out and read them to Phil and the girls, and I always ended up laughing until the tears rolled down my cheeks. One incident comes to mind when he wrote...

> A good friend of mine came to see me today and told me he was going on a trip to America. I told my friend I had a daughter who lived there with her family. I asked him, if he came anywhere near you, if he might drop by to see you. He asked me to describe you to him. I said you were the same height as the beloved Queen Victoria, of amiable disposition, and if all the perfume of all the American, sweet smelling flowers were poured on you, you couldn't be sweeter. I also told him if you go to her home, you will not find her drinking or smoking, but she will probably be knitting a sweater. When Mr. Winston Churchill returned from his visit to the United States, he came by again to tell me you had two of the prettiest girls in America, then he took one look at my old wizen clock and said, "I wonder where the youngsters get their beauty from."

This was just one of his more humorous letters, but many of them were quite serious on subjects such as the government being too lenient in its punishment of crimes, especially those committed by the young people. These things alone could fill a book. It's a pity he was never serious enough to have something published.

I think the last letter I got was one on the lighter side, telling me about his adventure as a film extra. A movie was being made on the Doncaster race course. The film focussed on the horses and the jockeys who rode them and the title was "The Rainbow Jacket." When Dad applied, he was given a bit part as one of the owner/trainers and because of his small stature and the way he was dressed, he really looked the part. This lasted several days, but on the first day when he went to collect his pay he said that was a true red-letter day for him because, as far back as he could remember, this was the first time he ever went home from the race course with money in his pocket.

Then he wrote that, he and Mother were receiving their old-age pension (social security) and were living very nicely in their retirement. Actually, because he was a World War I Veteran and had put in over three years of service overseas, he was entitled to a rent-free house with seven shillings per week thrown in. At that time there were over two million people receiving public assistance and then he said. . .

> "No Genty, I'm proud to say we are not among that number. We refused to accept assistance from anyone. Your mother is very kind to me in my declining years. I don't think she would like to lose her little Joseph yet, even if I do look like one of the ruins that Cromwell knocked about a bit. So, she deserves a final bow. May the Lord preserve you."
>
> Your loving Pop.

There was a P.S. directed to Heather. This was a quiz in English History. He would send the answer in his next letter. Sad to say, there were no more letters. Dad died shortly after in March 1956, at the age of 76. At his request, I was never told he was dying from cancer of the esophagus. He didn't want me to see him in his emaciated state caused by the disease.

I felt very bad about his passing. There was so much I wanted to tell him and to thank him for but I wanted to do it all in person. I especially wanted to thank him for helping me to walk. If I had never been able to walk, I certainly could never have gone dancing and I would have never met Phil.

Phil felt very bad, too. He was always going to send me back to see him, but I was the one who wanted to wait until we could afford for all of us to go together. I guess that was an incident when hindsight was better than foresight.

The following words were the quiz on English history concerning two eminent Statesmen:

Who wrote this?

"I would rather be a could be if I cannot be an are. For a could be is a maybe with a chance of touching par. I would rather be a has been than a might have been by far. For a might be is a hasn't been but a has was once an are."

We never did find the answer but I did, at one time, hear Mr. William Buckley, Jr. quote part of this on one of his TV shows. Maybe, sometime I might be brave enough to write and ask him.

The following year, Phil insisted I go to England and visit the rest of my family and relatives. This was Heather's senior year in high school, which was important to her, so she stayed home with Phil and I took Cathy with me. I realized later I had done the right thing even though Cathy got very sick. I guess the change of climate was bad for her. It was very cold and rained most of the time. My mother came to the rescue and took great care of her. Those were the last memories I had of my mother; she died in 1960.

I saw my sisters and brother and all of their families. Then we went to see Aunt Alice and Uncle Fred. Everyone was in total agreement that it was like seeing Heather again because Cathy looked so much like her, even at that age (she had just turned four). We went to see Dot and Joe Stenton. Their family had grown up. Sylvia was a lovely girl at age 17 and was in training to be a nurse. Unfortunately, she died at age 21 from a kidney disease which was a very sad blow for them.

Before Cathy and I left England, we went to see Phil's family. We stayed with his sister Edith. She and Jack now had two girls, Lesley and Betty. By this time Cathy was really homesick and missed Phil and Heather. Jack did his best to comfort her, and he tucked her in bed after a cup of hot chocolate each night. Phil's mother was in poor health at that time and a few years later she also passed away.

The Cake Box

It was now mid 1958, and Phil had worked downtown a little over five years, but it has always been his ambition to eventually go into business for himself. It came to his attention that a certain bakery was up for sale so he decided to look into it. This bakery was owned and operated by Lisle Bartlett. One of his employees was also interested in the sale.

Mr. Bartlett offered to let Phil work for him for a while to get the feel of the place and give him an insight into the business, so he accepted the offer. By the end of the year, Phil was convinced this was a good business. The location was good, the clientele was excellent, and Mr. Bartlett had a good reputation, especially among his employees.

However, neither the employee nor Phil had enough money for the down payment so they decided to go into the business as partners. The name was changed from Bartlett's to the Cake Box Bakery and the opening day was January 2, 1959.

On one side of us was a dry cleaners and on the other side was a grocery store, the owner of which was also our landlord. He owned the whole block of property. Because we had to sell our home in order to pay our share of the down payment, we were now living in a large apartment close to the bakery which was very convenient. This part of Spokane was, and still is, referred to as the South Hill and consists of many older but elegant homes and beautiful parks.

When the men took over the business they agreed to keep all of the same staff including sales people. They were a motley crew and got along well together. Some of the regular customers were a little skeptical about the changes at first, but it didn't take long for them to come around.

For the most part the bakers stuck to their usual routine of making the many varieties of bread, Danish sweet roles, doughnuts, etc. Lisle Bartlett had not done much in the cake business so Phil decided to concentrate on that line and went all out for it. He soon built up a good reputation.

I had learned a lot about the business from Phil over the years, but since I had never worked in a bakery, Mr. Bartlett was able to give me a lot of advice, and with help from the staff, I managed to get into the routine of things.

We had a very good accountant, named Sam Farber. He helped with the bookkeeping and assured us the first three years were quite successful so we were all encouraged. Unfortunately, during the last year, we were informed by the landlord that he was intending to do some remodeling.

He was going to remove some houses from around the block and build a small supermarket with lots of parking space. His grocery store, the bakery, and the cleaners would all be turned into a large drug store then the bakery and the cleaners would be added on to the side of the supermarket.

This would mean a big expense for us. Moving equipment was very costly although, actually, some of ours was very old and wasn't worth the expense of moving. Because this move was made to look very progressive, Phil and his partner decided it would be cheaper in the long run to buy all new equipment. This of course was a problem since they were still paying for the business. A good friend of ours, who was also our insurance agent, offered to lend us the money at 7% interest. This was in the amount of $18,000.

Everything sounded very good until we found out when the two partners signed a new lease for five years they would be paying rent to a new landlord. It seems the former landlord had arranged the sale of the supermarket even before it was completed, without notifying Phil and his partner. Because they had already bought the new equipment, there was no turning back, they had no practical choice at this point.

Their reason for being angry and disappointed was the fact that the supermarket was not up to the standard of quality which the small grocery store had always maintained for years.

The bakery rent was raised and a short time after the new grand opening took place, Phil's partner pulled out. From then on, Phil was the sole owner.

He was determined not to let this turn of events beat him. So he proceeded to do the best he could under the circumstances, and for a while it was quite a struggle. It was very different from running a grocery store where you just reach for an item from a shelf. Every item in a bakery has to be made first, and Phil always used the best quality ingredients. Also, it was a union bakery and we paid full scale union wages plus health, welfare, and pension plan benefits for the bakers.

We continued to work hard and during those years Heather helped not only at the bakery but at home as well. Someone had to be there when Cathy got home from school. We managed to hold on to our good clientele. They stayed very loyal to us, and although it was difficult at times, I really enjoyed working alongside Phil.

I thought I had seen everything before we were married, when Phil turned my mother's kitchen into a small bakery, but he still never failed to amaze me with the variety of things he made. I made it my responsibility to display as much as I could in the store window, then took a look from the outside, which always gave me a feeling of pride.

I soon learned to do something different for every special occasion like Easter, Halloween, and so forth. This was always fun for the children, but I think Christmas was my favourite. We made large coffee cakes in the shape of a tree which were very popular. These would be decorated with white frosting, red and green glazed cherries for ornaments, and sprinkled with silver dragées depicting the lights. These were the type of things Heather worked on, but she also became very efficient in cake icing, too.

The cookie business was fantastic because of the many varieties like Pfeffernuesse, Springerle, Divinity, Spritz, and the many Christmas shapes of sugar cookies sprinkled with different colored sugar.

I will always remember a certain gentlemen, the Rev. Dorpat, who seemed to sense exactly just what time to drop in. He would open the door and wait a few seconds until the aroma of anise would drift toward his nose, then he would declare in a loud voice, "Ah, Springerle!" It was almost as if he found a long lost tradition.

There was also a very special lady, Mrs. Rosalie Tubbs. She said no one made Springerle that turned out looking "Picture Perfect" the way they are supposed to look, no one that is, except Phil.

Another one of his specialties was fruit cake. We always sold a lot at Christmas and Thanksgiving. It was made with about 90% fruit and 10% cake batter and the fruit was soaked in brandy and muscatel for a week. Just the smell of this sold the cake and it kept indefinitely.

I think the main attraction at Christmas time was the beautiful gingerbread houses. Phil could never make enough to meet the demand. They were very time consuming and a true labor of love. I was able to help decorate them, but it was Phil's artistic touch, with the delicate icicles, that made them so special. I can see the children now with their noses pressed against the window and their eyes wide open in wonderment. These fun houses were usually surrounded by gingerbread men with their colorful buttons and bow ties.

There's no doubt this was the busiest time of the year and quite a challenge to all the bakers, especially when it came to making all the many types of dinner rolls and party breads and pies. We had to use a number system at these times as well as every Sunday morning for that matter. There was always a rush after every Church service when the customers would bring in their children and let them choose their own treats. We really did enjoy a pleasant business relationship with these families which was very gratifying.

We met some good neighbors in this vicinity but I wasn't able to mix with them very often. However, Cathy spent a lot of time with her school friends, and as I recall, from the time she was very small she seemed drawn to older people. Therefore, it was not surprising when she struck up what turned out to be a lasting friendship with Mrs. Olive Marshall. Olive was a retired English teacher, turned writer, and she became a big influence on Cathy. She was always pushing her to the limits when it came to her schooling.

This was the era of the Beatles, and like all her friends, Cathy had a crush on the fabulous four. Her favourite was Paul McCartney and when it came time for his birthday, Phil had to make a special cake. To top it all, when the group came to Vancouver, B.C., Cathy pestered us to let her go to see them in person. We finally gave in on the condition she worked at the bakery to pay for a ticket. Of course, I couldn't let a twelve year old go alone, so I agreed to go with her (perish the thought). I was really surprised when Olive wanted to go with us.

All the way to Canada on the bus, Olive kept repeating that, because I was used to finding safe places during the bombing raids in the war, she was sure I would know where we would be safe during the concert, just in case their was rowdy behavior. I thought that was funny, but I remember Olive wrote an article about our adventure later.

As the years passed, the supermarket changed hands again and Phil was getting tired of their so-called business tactics and false advertising. He made up his mind to move when the lease was up in February 1967.

Until that time, we continued to struggle. I have to say that Phil was not a businessman. Even worse, he was generous to a fault. Sometimes he reminded me of an artist who jealously guarded his work, but if we were ever going to pay off that loan, I would have to be the business head and handle the situation as best I could.

Before we made the move, Heather took a trip to Europe and she liked Italy so well she decided to stay there and work her way around. While she was in Genoa, she met the love of her life, a young man named Ernesto Leveque. So she continued to work there for over a year.

Ernesto was born in Rome and worked as a conductor on the trains which travelled through Europe. He spoke several languages, but he knew very little English. On the other hand, Heather could now speak Italian fluently so they were able to communicate. In June 1965, they were married in Genoa and came back to the United States to start their married life together.

Soon after they arrived in Spokane, we gave them a very nice wedding reception at the Golden Hour Restaurant. Of course, Phil made a beautiful three, tier wedding cake. Around the center of the top tier, he placed a strip of silver foil (the war souvenirs I spoke of earlier). We had saved it for all those years. I thought, at that time, how ironic that something which had caused such havoc was now part of a centerpiece of such a happy occasion.

We put Ernesto to work in the bakery, for the time being, until he could work out what was best for them. He stayed with us for quite some time and adapted to baking very well. He was a good, conscientious worker.

They had three children close together. This, I'm sure, Heather thought was better than having gone thirteen years like we did before she had a sister. She was a much better mother than I ever was and Ernesto was a good father, strict with good morals but very loving. Alessandro Philip was their first child, then Simonetta Silvia, and Cristina Luciana. Eventually, we notified all of the staff of our intentions to relocate so they would be prepared, but as it so happened, two of them were retiring and the others got work elsewhere. That just left Ernesto and Cammy our pretty, petite sales girl, to go along with us.

The North Side

When we did move in 1967, it was over to the north side. This area wasn't as large in comparison to the South Hill so we got by with a smaller place and less help. We managed to draw a good clientele and many of our loyal customers made the trip all the way across town or called on their way to the Country Club, so we were never wanting for business. Again, this was a costly move, but as always Phil worked all hours and finally our loan was paid off.

It was while we were here that a lady came in and introduced herself as, Kay Deslaurier. She was originally from Aldershot in England. Her husband, Irv, was Canadian. When their daughter, Jan, was married, we made the wedding cake and from then on we became very close friends.

Cathy was now in Mead High School and later in the fall of 1970 she met the love of her life, Jeff McAlister. He had asked Cathy to the homecoming dance and that was the start of their romantic courtship. Jeff was a great athlete. He played football but he really excelled in basketball.

Ernesto, who was a great lover of soccer, was one of the first few to get the game started in Spokane. He particularly enjoyed getting a team of little kids together, including his young son Sandro. He eventually was involved with coaching soccer in high school and refereeing.

During all these years we never had a vacation, but on occasion Phil did manage to go fishing. His favourite place was high up in the Cascade Mountains at a place called Trapper Lake. Phil would drive to Lake Chelan, about 150 miles from Spokane, and from there would go by float plane. The well known pilot of the plane, Ernie Gibson, made daily trips to Stehekin, then higher up to Trapper which was a glacial lake. Because Trapper was only open for about two months out of each year, these trips were limited and they were restricted to three days. Phil looked on this part of the state as his real Shangrila. It was so relaxing for him. He took a few of his fishing buddies from time to time.

I went with him once. Even though I'm afraid of the water, once I got on that rubber raft, I never gave it a second thought. That is until we rowed across to the other side of the lake to get some ice. Phil took his axe to break off a chunk of ice and the axe slipped from his hand and made a hole in the raft. I didn't have sense enough to realize there was a sausage around the raft so we wouldn't drown and I was very scared. I think even the marmots, living around the lake, had a good laugh about that one.

Ernesto got to go on one of these trips, too, but I think Phil was most pleased when Cathy agreed to go with him. Cathy was 15 years old at the time. Phil said her Camp Fire Girls experience served her well. The first thing she did, after helping him with the tent, was to dig a hole for a pottie and drive a wooden stake to hold a toilet roll.

Around this time, she was acting like a real teenage brat, which I'm sure was supposed to be normal, although we could never excuse it. Quite some time later I discovered, among some of her school work, something that she had written about her trip with Phil. She got top marks for her efforts. It went like this . . .

> Even though I get a lot of razz from the boys, I will freely admit I like to go fishing. I really get a thrill out of having those wiggly things tug at my line. But when my dad asked me to go on a fishing trip with him to a little lake in the mountains where you had to fly in, I sure had some reservations. I like to fish, yes, but for three full days! And I had never flown before and we would be landing on water! Nobody would be near us for a least fifteen miles. I knew

this wasn't for me but I figured it was my duty to go. It was either me go or my dad wouldn't go at all.

I was trying to show I wasn't nervous on the plane but my dad knew the look on my face all too well. It was one of those "I wish I didn't have to go through with this" looks. I could almost feel the blood surging downward from my head and then my head was a helium balloon. I could visualize some little kid with a string tied around his wrist with me on the end of it, floating around--and then he lets go.

Before I knew it, we had landed. I took one look and to think I almost didn't come. My dad hadn't mentioned any glaciers or waterfalls or wild flowers, anything like this. He just said a fishing trip. Now I knew why he had wanted to come so bad. I actually had goose bumps. I had never gotten them before just by looking at wilderness. I thought God himself had to live in a place this beautiful. Suddenly, thunder broke in a loud crash. Part of one of the glaciers had broken off and dove into the water. About five minutes later, there were swells of water coming up to the shore and waves grabbed the rocks around us. They hadn't come from across the lake but from down, deep, underneath where the piece of glacier had forced the water out of its now occupied space.

Everything was so green, green as you hear Ireland is supposed to be. The water was so clear and fresh, fresh enough to stick my mouth in and drink. I found out what glacier water is like, very cold and smooth.

I kept saying that I couldn't believe this place. I felt it was all my own and no one else

> had seen it before. I didn't think my dad was as touched as I, but he was acting like such a different person. His deep gray eyes were opened so wide and he wasn't listening to anything I said. I realized then that I wasn't going to have any problem fishing for three days. My problem was going to be leaving.

After reading it, I knew we hadn't created a monster after all. They went a second time in 1969, and during the trip Neil Armstrong walked on the moon. To celebrate this event, Cathy carved their names and the date on a tree.

Those years on the north side of town went along smoothly, but Phil's mind was often focused on the future. Therefore, it was with mutual consent that Ernesto found himself another job with a good commercial bakery. He has stayed with the same firm ever since. We didn't have to worry about Cammy, she and Bill Yeend were married and they moved to Seattle.

However, Phil was looking for something different. As we drew close to the end of our five year lease, we learned there would be a raise in our rent and possibly a percentage of our sales. Phil didn't want to take this route anymore so he decided to take another direction by going into specializing in wedding and special occasion cakes only. Of course, this meant another move but it wouldn't be so costly this time. First we would search for a home in the right zoning area for a home occupation. This was easier said than done. It took quite a while but since our landlord had no other tenant lined up, he was good enough to let us stay on until we found something suitable.

Finally, we found just the right location and a neat brick home. Even though it was not quite finished, we were able to move in. This was on Country Homes Boulevard and still on the north side. The first thing Phil did was to invite the state health inspector to help him plan the bakery in the basement, which was at ground level. Our living quarters were on the upper level. The house was terraced and sat at an angle on the side of a small hill so we were able to arrange a half circular driveway for easy access and a double garage which would lead into the bakery. We sold the equipment that we didn't need and moved the rest into its new quarters. Now, in June 1972, we had a brand new home and a new style of business.

I would like to say that this was Phil's cup of tea but it was more than that. It was the first time we had made any real amount of money and were able to put money in the bank. Everything was now under one roof, with just one payment. Many customers were disappointed that we stopped producing all the other goodies, especially the bread. We had to explain many times, there was never any money made on a good loaf of bread and we had to start being practical.

We were both amazed at the amount of business that came along immediately. It was the height of the wedding season and Phil was having to turn orders down, much to his dismay. He only had one pair of hands. The only thing that I could help him with was weighing and sifting the flour and powdered sugar. This job didn't bother me, but I know it bothered him. I also greased most of the cake pans. I often belittled my small contribution, but he always said that he could not have made it without me.

Most of my time was now spent with something I wouldn't dare call working, only a pleasure. It was a most rewarding experience and a lot of fun. I had my own separate room next to Phil's work room where I took orders and interviewed the bride-to-be. This room was nicely decorated and I always had a large selection of ornaments for the top of the cakes. We also used fresh flowers whenever preferred.

The young ladies would sit around with their mother or friends and we would discuss the size of their wedding, the type of cake, etc. They usually brought in a swatch of material from the bridesmaids' dresses so that Phil could carry out the color scheme on the cake. I met a lot of lovely girls and felt privileged to be a part of their weddings.

Usually the conversation would get around to the young lady's engagement ring and I saw many beautiful diamonds. I would bring my hand close to compare my tiny ring and tell them how old it was. I also would show them that my wedding ring was engraved with a minute scroll all the way around. Phil was able to copy that scroll onto the cakes which became one of his many trademarks. When I told this story, they thought it was quite romantic and I was often urged to write a book about it. I always said that maybe one day I would.

I always went with him on deliveries, mainly to map out directions, not for any famous short cuts but for the best route with the smoothest ride for the cakes. I don't think there was a church in Spokane that we didn't deliver a cake to, as well as some beautiful outdoor home receptions.

We got good business from all the big hotels, the Country Clubs, etc. One day when we went to the City Club, I heard Phil thanking the head chef, Dave Gross, for the business. Dave replied, "It works both ways Phil. You want the business and I want the best for my club."

These were great years for Phil. He was sought out by the cream of society, and rightly so.

By this time Cathy and Jeff were attending Eastern Washington State College. Jeff was on the basketball team, the "Screamin' Eagles," so we made an effort to watch his games whenever possible. Jeff helped us with our yard work as Phil never liked gardening. For as long as we were in that house, Jeff was our gardener and sometimes he helped with cake deliveries.

We had a huge rock in front of the house. I remember the first time our friend, Kay Deslaurier, saw it. She thought it was beautiful. She always did have a green thumb and had creative landscaping ideas for this very unwanted rock. Phil told her it was all hers, she could do whatever she liked with it. He wanted no part of it.

Kay came to have lunch with us every Wednesday. Being from England, we had a lot in common. Like me, she was crazy about knitting. Being fully aware of Phil's sense of humor, she was never surprised when she got home at what he had slipped into her shopping bag. I remember one time it was a one pound weight.

Spokane was the site for Expo 1974 so the city was buzzing. It was also the year of Cathy and Jeff's wedding. They were married in St. John's Cathedral where Cathy was baptized. This is also the Cathedral where they have the bells which produce the beautiful sounding carillon chime. These bells were cast in Loughborough, England by the Taylor Brothers and sent to the United States, especially for this Cathedral of St. John.

The place for their wedding reception was a gift from Gerry and Doris Larson. They owned what is now a restaurant called Patsy Clark's Mansion, but at the time was the Francis Lester Inn. This had been a beautiful place years ago but was run down when they bought it. Gerry was in the construction business so he and Doris did wonders in restoring it to its original splendor. They were also able to retrieve many of the antiques that were lost from time to time.

The Larsons held all kinds of receptions at the Francis Lester Inn, and we supplied them with most of the wedding cakes. They closed temporarily during the exposition in order to arrange guided tours so that the public could see and appreciate its beauty once again. However, they did make an exception and opened for Cathy and Jeff's wedding reception. Later on they sold the place, and it was then made into a restaurant.

In September of that year, my Aunt Jessie, who had been widowed twice, died suddenly. When I went up to Canada for her funeral, I was surprised to find that her brother, my Uncle Edmund, was in the Shaughnessy Veteran's Hospital.

The day before the funeral I received a phone call from a lady who said she was a friend of my aunt. For proof of this she said that her children now had the gingerbread house which we had given to my aunt years ago. This lady was a complete stranger to me, but she invited me to her home for dinner that night. The day that I entered the home of Nell and Ed McCormick was one of my most memorable moments. They were as Irish as St. Patrick himself, and when I sat down at their large dinner table, surrounded by six children, the warmth that I felt inside of me was truly overwhelming.

I remember the meal to this day; the good home-cooked chicken and dumplings, but it was obvious to me that food was not the only thing served to those children. They each got a large portion of the most important thing a family needs today--LOVE.

I couldn't help notice that they had a Wurlitzer organ. I knew it had to be special, and I'm sure it must have been a great financial sacrifice for them to buy it. When they asked if I would like to hear young Ed play, I soon found out how special this organ was. I was spellbound when I heard the performance of this young boy.

It seems that young Ed used to walk into this music store every day and hang around the organs wishing that he could play them. Finally, he got his wish and the owner gave him music lessons in exchange for working around the store. His Father also played a little while we all sang mostly Irish popular songs.

I couldn't wait to phone Phil and tell him about my wonderful evening. Before I left, Mrs. McCormick told me she worked at Grace Hospital which was next to the Veteran's Hospital. She offered to look in on my uncle from time to time and would let me know when she thought his time was near. I had known for some time he was suffering from cancer in his throat but he had managed to stay home until now.

I got a call on Christmas day that Uncle Edmund had taken a turn for the worse. We had just finished dinner, so I dropped everything and Phil drove me to the airport. I stayed with my uncle at the hospital because he was very alert. He wasn't very big, but he was a tough old bird. He died two days later. The McCormicks came to his funeral, and they allowed young Ed to play organ music during the service, which I thought was a nice gesture.

The McCormicks are now living in comfortable retirement on Vancouver Island in British Columbia and I have kept in touch with them. Many times they have been a great source of comfort to me, especially in later years.

In late 1975, Phil and I decided to take a trip. We hadn't had a real vacation in years. I was still trying to persuade him to go to England, he hadn't been back since we left, but I couldn't convince him. When some friends mentioned that we should go to Hawaii, Phil seemed to like the idea, especially since my Uncle Edmund had left us a little money in his will.

First we bought a new Chrysler Town and Country wagon for the business and we still had enough funds to pay for a trip. We took off at the end of September for ten days. We had a wonderful time. We were like newlyweds again. This was definitely the honeymoon we were deprived of years ago.

We were not at all impressed with the commercialism, but we were very inspired by the beauty and culture of the Island. We found ourselves in a different world of fantasy and romance. We felt young, and we fell in love all over again. As I sat on the beach of this tropical paradise, I watched Phil walking toward the ocean where he was able to swim to his heart's content. I thought to myself that, even at sixty years old, he had a great pair of legs and still looked good in bathing trunks.

After we came back down to earth and we were on our way home, he reminded me of the poet Browning's words, "Grow old along with me, the best is yet to be." He also said, "You know Jess, we have both worked so hard for so long, we owe this much to ourselves." I told him I couldn't agree more.

We continued to enjoy our new working arrangement. We saw our grandchildren more often. I admired Heather for the way she managed them, especially since Ernesto always worked the night shift. They were all in school but loved to come over and watch Phil at work, especially when it was a cake for their birthday. I also admired her in that when she was twenty-one she chose to be baptized into the Catholic Church. Our good friend Nina Trump was her God Mother. Heather remained steadfast in her faith, and Nina was always an important part of her life.

It was now 1976, the year of the Bicentennial of the independence of the United States. This made for a busy time for everyone. We had a lot more weddings than we normally had and many cakes for patriotic events.

We had always made cakes for the Lincoln Savings and Loan Bank on President Lincoln's birthday, but this year they requested something extra special. Phil came up with a real masterpiece. He made a large sheet cake on which he drew the American eagle in relief with ribbon in its beak and the inscription E PLURIBUS UNUM printed on the ribbon. There was a log cabin placed on the side and also a bust of the famous President with the words MARTYR OF FREEDOM just below the bust. All around the edges of the cake were shields on which he drew the five stars and thirteen stripes. It looked truly magnificent, carried out in the traditional colors of red, white and blue.

Phil reminded me to check our schedule so we could plan our trip to Hawaii again. I found we had a break at the end of August so I went ahead and booked with the travel agent. Cathy and Jeff would go along this time. It would be a delayed honeymoon for them, and they planned to go to Maui for a few days and then join us later in Waikiki. We were more than ready when the time arrived.

As we boarded the plane, we had no idea of the surprise that was in store for us. After we were airborne for a while, the stewardess came along and asked what we would prefer for our meal, chicken or salmon. However, she neglected to say Chicken Almondine and Phil was allergic to almonds.

We both chose the chicken. Phil took a couple of bites from that food and passed out like a light. He was given oxygen immediately, but because of confined seating he couldn't breathe and passed out again. His throat was starting to swell and he panicked. A doctor was called for and Phil spent the rest of the flight on the floor in the first-class compartment with the doctor close by. Luckily he had the right medication with him to treat Phil's allergy so he was fine by the time we reached Honolulu. The airline personnel insisted on having an ambulance waiting to take him to the emergency, just to check him over. If we had been superstitious we would have sworn this was a bad omen, but we put the incident aside temporarily.

The next day we went down to the beach early, and we met a nice elderly couple who spoke with a strong Brooklyn accent. They seemed eager to befriend us and wanted to drive us around the Island so we arranged to meet them the following day. They were as good as their word so we had an enjoyable day with Sara and Dan Collins. They certainly knew where to find the nicest beaches and the best places to eat.

During lunch I brought up the incident about Phil on the plane, and Sara asked who the doctor was that checked him over. I told her it was Dr. Scott, and she smiled and said she knew him very well and that he was a good doctor. Sara told us that his mother was also a doctor and she knew her too.

A few days later Cathy and Jeff joined us. Phil spent most of the time swimming with them while I was content to sit in the shade of the small palm trees. The day before they left we were all strolling down Kalakaua Avenue trying to decide where to have lunch and we came to the newly built twin towers of the Hyatt Regency. We went into the lobby and looked around for the restaurants and Phil was drawn by the display of wonderful looking pastries.

After lunch he said, quite casually, that it would be great to work at a place like this in the winters. Then just as casually he said, "Wait here and I'll see if they need any help." We all thought he was joking. He was gone about ten minutes and when he came back he said, "How soon can I start?" Apparently the hotel had only recently finished their bakery, which supplied their restaurants, and they were short of help. Phil told them he would think about it, but he didn't mention it again until Cathy and Jeff left for home.

We made the most of the few days we had left in this trip to Hawaii. We also met our friends, Sara and Dan, once more and we told them about Phil being offered this job. They thought that was great and hoped he would accept.

On the way home, Phil was very quiet, but I knew what was going through his mind. Suddenly he asked, "What do you think about me taking the job?"

I told him, "If you are really serious we should talk it over with the family when we got home." After we settled back into our work, we did discuss this matter further.

Phil always enjoyed his work at any time or place with the exception of delivering the wedding cakes in the hazardous, wintry weather. The summer was a breeze, but those winters were very nerve racking. It wasn't the driving but the many steps up and down to the churches, hotels, or whatever. They were not always free from ice and snow. Heaven forbid that anything should happen to his cakes. If he ever let anyone down, it certainly would be a catastrophe. I can see him now pacing back and forth with one eye on the snow storm and the other on the clock. I often wondered how he managed to survive these situations, but somehow he always did.

Now I understood why he was debating over this opportunity to get away and avoid those cold weather deliveries that had become a thorn in his side. Phil also explained that he thought it would be nice for both of us to be away from the cold weather and get outside more by working for someone else. We could then go back to Spokane, in the summer, for the busy wedding season.

It all sounded feasible to me and I didn't want to dampen his spirits so I went along with his idea that we at least give it a try. First of all we would take care of all our commitments, orders that ran to the middle of October. Then we would let it be known that we would be closed for business until further notice. If our plan didn't work, we could always come back.

The only thing we weren't sure of was our home. We knew it wasn't exactly what we had in mind at the time we made the purchase, but we were told it had good resale value so we looked upon it as an investment. We decided to put it up for sale, and if we came back from Hawaii, we would take plenty of time before we chose our next location. Heather would be in charge of things while we were away, and Jeff would keep up with the yard work.

Real estate was slow moving at that time so we didn't expect much in the way of buyers for a while. Phil phoned the manager of the hotel to tell him he was accepting the offer of a job and would be there around mid October.

When we were finally on our way. I remember thinking, "another move." It didn't bother me because I had said years ago that I would follow him to the ends of the earth. Now, it looked as though I was on my way to doing just that.

PREFACE
PART TWO

"THE VICIOUS CIRCLE"

Before I continue, I would like to explain that with the exception of a few, the names of the people mentioned from here on have been changed to protect their privacy.

I also wish to say that I have no desire to discredit any of the doctors regarding the qualifications of their respective professions. I am sure everyone did whatever they thought was best for my husband and I realize they cannot perform miracles.

My complaints are directed toward the few who saw fit to intimidate and/or patronize me at such times when I felt so helpless and was too timid to speak out in my own defense.

However, as the years went by, I grew stronger and I will defend to my dying day the right to have done whatever I thought was necessary to seek help whenever possible. I sought out the doctors with only one purpose in mind. It was simply in the hope that any one of them would be able to at least relieve or come up with some form of treatment for my husband's damaged brain.

I also want to stress the fact that I am not condemning the flu vaccines or any other vaccine, especially those for children. I realize they are beneficial and almost imperative in some instances. However, for the percentage of people who would fall in the same category as my husband, I definitely feel there is a need for a more aggressive type of warning on consent forms. In this way, these people would have a better understanding of the dangers before proceeding.

Hawaii and the Flu Vaccines

Phil was to start work at the Hyatt on October 19. He would work five days and then get two days off. Our new friends (the Collins) insisted on helping us look for a place to live. We found a very nice condominium, small, but quite reasonable, and fully furnished.

I arranged to meet Phil when he got off work his first day. He worked from 3:00 a.m. to noon. After work he went for a swim and then we ate lunch together before going home.

He was so happy and very impressed with the quality of pastry chefs he came in contact with. He told me he would be working overtime for a while. They were so busy, and in spite of all the help, were not fully organized.

On Phil's first day off, he spent the day just relaxing and that evening we went out for dinner to celebrate his first successful week. On the second day, Monday, October 25, Sara and Dan came around to remind us of the immunization program taking place at Blaidsdell Center.

Because of a possibility of an outbreak of Swine Flu, the vaccine was being offered as a precaution and to prevent any spreading of the disease. It had been brought to the attention of the public that this Swine Flu was similar to a virus which had killed thousands of people during the first World War. Consequently, President Ford was shown on television earlier in the year taking the shot and urging everyone to do the same.

When Sara told us that their doctor friends advised them to have the shots, we went along with the expert advise and rode in their car to get the shots at the same time. I remember the shots were given using a gun method rather than with a needle.

Apparently, after questioning, Phil, was advised to have a shot of the A/Victoria Flu vaccine, also. This surprised me in that I wasn't aware of this until we got back to the hotel and he showed me the consent forms which he had signed, one blue and one white. I know now, only to well, on that day we had made the biggest mistake of our entire life.

We were looking forward to moving into the condominium in a few days where we could be more comfortable. The very next day, which started Phil's second week, I went to meet him on the beach again at lunch time and he was fine. However, on the Wednesday it was a different story. He didn't feel like eating, had a headache and was coughing and sneezing. His nose was a constant drip. We thought he just had a cold and treated the symptoms with cough drops and aspirins. Before the day was over, he was running a temperature.

By Friday he was no better and what's more, he came home limping and he said, "Good grief, what the hell next is going to happen to me! My foot is killing me!"

It was a big relief when he took his shoe off, but from the instep all the way down, including his toes, there was swelling. There was no bruising, just numbness. I found him some old sneakers and cut part of the top away to keep the pressure off his foot. He was determined not to stay home from work. On his next two days off, he would be able to rest and then he would be OK, or so he thought.

The following week was no better and I wanted him to see a doctor, but he kept telling me to stop worrying. He was sure he would get over this so-called cold. I did get him to see a foot doctor and the x-rays showed nothing except what we already knew, he had a bunion. Phil said he told the doctor he had dropped a lawn mower on his foot and evidently he believed him because he wrote that in his report. I asked him why he made such a joke because he never even went near a lawn mower.

We received a phone call from Heather to say that someone was interested in our home, and were we prepared to let it go at this time? We were surprised, to say the least, but Phil thought I should go home and deal with the prospective buyer while he kept on working. I told him I would only go on the condition that he went to see Dr. Scott. Phil promised me he would. I wanted him to phone me and tell me what the doctor had to say.

This was about the middle of November. I flew home to Spokane and was there eight days. I met with the real estate people who assured me they had a positive buyer for our home. As it turned out, I did the right thing in letting it go. During that time I gave things to our two daughters. They helped me with a yard sale of years of accumulation. I then put the remains of our belongings and our car into storage.

Phil phoned me but he couldn't do the talking because, by now, his throat was so bad that he had lost his voice. Sara spoke for him and said not to worry, she and Dan would keep an eye on him until I got back. Sara also told me Dr. Scott diagnosed Phil as having chronic asthma and bronchitis.

When I did get back they were all at the airport to meet me. Sara had made a beautiful lei from the sweet smelling plumaria and gave it to Phil to put around my neck. He was so happy to have me back, but he sounded terrible.

I finally persuaded him to stay away from work until he felt better. I phoned the hotel bakery and explained that Phil wasn't able to speak for himself but he was intending to get back to work as soon as possible. Unfortunately, he never did get back. He never got better, and I was starting to get very worried.

I mentioned the flu shots a couple of times, but Phil just shook his head and said that he didn't think that was the cause of his sickness. I asked him if Dr. Scott had brought the subject up and he said that the doctor knew we both had the shots and was sure he would tell us if there was any cause for alarm.

Phil was now beginning to lose weight fast. His cough was much worse, and he was short of breath most of the time. He went to see Dr. Scott again in December and his diagnosis was the same. He continued to give him medication for progressive asthmatic exacerbation. He was treated with steroid injections, prednisone by mouth, penicillin injections and various medi-halers. Even with all of this medication there was little relief. I felt so bad for him. He hardly went outside, and it wasn't fun going swimming anymore. He couldn't stand not being able to work. He was like a fish out of water.

I told Dr. Scott that we were aware of Phil's form of asthma or catarrh, as we called it, which seemed to affect his nasal passages. I also told him that, over the years, he was usually given penicillin shots and some kind of medi-halers and that seemed to take care of it. Phil was never off work and was never hospitalized for the condition. He had never been this bad before.

I hated to say this to Phil but I had a feeling his plans just weren't going to work out. When I suggested we ought to think about going back to Spokane, he got very upset. He kept reminding me that we made a decision to give this venture a try, so he wanted to wait until he got better to give it a fair try.

I was having many doubts and I think deep down that he was too. He just didn't want to admit that fact, yet. He wanted so badly to go back to his job at the hotel, but in his present condition, it wasn't the right thing to do. Every few minutes he would have to stop the nasal drip or a coughing spell. A box of kleenex tissues was out of the question. It was simply pockets full of wet handkerchiefs. This would not only be bad for his fellow workers but even worse from a health standard, especially around food. I'm sure it would have been an embarrassing situation all around.

I did promise Phil that I would stay there with him. He deserved that much, at the very least. Besides, it might be a better idea to try and encourage him to get plenty of sun instead of rushing home to the cold and snow in Spokane.

Just before Christmas I persuaded him to go for a walk and as we came to the Kuhio Theatre, I thought I recognized a familiar face. I had never met this man, but I had seen a picture of him. A friend and customer of ours and her husband asked if we would drop by the movie theatre and say hello to the manager who was of friend of theirs. We went up and introduced ourselves to this distinguished looking gentleman. After we talked about Phil's situation, this man asked if Phil would like to work for him as a door man. He told Phil that he wouldn't get rich, but it would give him something to do, and he would be outside most of the time. Phil jumped at the opportunity. He didn't care about the pay. The main thing is that he would be making himself useful.

They didn't have a uniform to fit him, but he had brought a good black suit from home. With a white shirt and tie, he felt a little more dressed for the part. I was OK with this arrangement except that when Phil was through in the evenings, he would sit on the side of the bed and cough so hard I thought he would choke.

We lived quite close to the theatre and one day the manager said to me he hoped Phil would stay on with them. He had made a big hit with the staff. He also said that because of his personality and the courteous way he greeted the patrons, he would like to train him to be a manager. He said he would then earn real money. I didn't know what to say except we had to get him feeling better before he could decide on anything.

During all of this time I had some minor problems myself, but I was so wrapped up in Phil's dilemma that I never brought it up. Every once in a while I would get a strange feeling in my toes and the balls of my feet, almost like cramping. I would be in a store or walking home with groceries when it would come on suddenly and my feet felt numb. I stopped once on the street and put my bags down while I took my sandals off and tried rubbing my toes. A gentleman came up and insisted on carrying the groceries home for me. When I got home I sat down and rubbed my feet again. They were tingling so bad and started to swell. The next day the same thing happened to my fingers. The inner sides were red and swollen. This happened several times and I couldn't figure out why.

Christmas day arrived, but I have to admit that it was totally different from what we had been used to. Sara and Dan encouraged us to have dinner with them at the Mirra Mar Hotel. This would be at noon because Phil was working the afternoon and evening shows. Christmas trees were on short supply in Hawaii so I used my imagination and decorated the chandeliers in the condo and strung Christmas cards all around. It was better than nothing. I thought it might give Phil a little Christmas spirit.

About mid January, 1977, I phoned Heather to tell her we had received payment for the sale of our home. I also told her we would probably be going back to Spokane sooner than we had planned, unless some kind of miracle occurred. Heather said we could stay with her whenever we decided to go until we could make other arrangements.

Phil continued to work at the theater, but one night when he came home, about midnight on the evening of February 9, he wasn't feeling good so he went straight to bed. About an hour later he started coughing hard. He just kept it up incessantly while, at the same time, fighting for his breath. Finally he got up and I made him comfortable in a chair hoping this would help. Suddenly he collapsed to the floor, unconscious. This was around 2:00 a.m., I phoned 911 and the paramedics arrived very quickly, but Phil was still unconscious. While one young man was preparing something to inject, the other was on the phone to emergency at the hospital. He turned quickly and said, "Hold the shot until we get to the hospital." I remember clearly the young man with the needle saying, "Jesus Christ, am I supposed to let the man die before we get him there." With that, he threw the needle across the room in sheer frustration. They placed him on the stretcher and I left with them in the ambulance. When they arrived at emergency, they gave him medication and then set up an intravenous infusion and told me I could wait there with him. I think we were there about four hours. Phil was feeling somewhat better so the doctor sent him home. He impressed on me that if Phil had another attack, to get him to the hospital right away.

This came sooner than I expected. At 4:30 p.m. that same day (February 10) I had to call 911 and this time they kept him in the hospital. They did all kinds of testing the next day and on the Saturday his doctor said, "I'm afraid Phil's lungs are badly damaged, and it looks like he has emphysema." He added, "Do you want me to contact a specialist to see Phil because he is not responding to any medication."

I told him, "Go ahead," so it was arranged.

I saw Dr. Michaels (the specialist) at the beginning of the next week and was relieved when he told me Phil did not have emphysema. I asked him about pneumonia and he said, "I have not ruled out that possibility, but for now, I am going to give him something that will get him out of the hospital by the weeks end."

I learned that the previous night Phil had been very depressed and talked about going home. His feet had begun to swell again but there was no pain, just a tingling sensation so the nurses tried to keep them elevated. I had given Sara's phone number to the hospital and during the early hours of the next morning she phoned me. She said not to be afraid because Phil was OK, but apparently he had been acting strange. He had walked into the nurses station with his IV bottle in hand and said it was gasoline, and if they didn't let him go home he was going to blow the place up.

The nurses then phoned Sara and persuaded Phil to talk to her. Sara told me that Phil kept saying they were holding him there against his will. However, she was able to talk him into going back to bed and she thought the medication was responsible for his actions. I was too upset to go back to bed so as soon as it was daylight I went to the hospital.

The first person I ran in to at the hospital was Dr. Scott and he asked, "Is Phil a violent man?"

"No, he is just the reverse," I answered.

Then he said, "I will have to cut down on the medication that Phil is taking," but he didn't say what the medication was. I learned later that he was being given prednisone.

When I went to the nurses station they all told me Phil had been apologizing to everyone after they told him about his behavior. They also told me he had been crying and was afraid of dying during the night. I knew he must have been hallucinating.

Phil was discharged from the hospital on February 19, and Dr. Scott advised him not to go back to work, not even to the theatre. He was given several prescriptions for prednisone, choledyl and for bronchosol and isoetharine for his "Maxi Mist" machine. He was advised to purchase this small breathing machine which he had to use constantly after he left the hospital.

We got a pleasant surprise when a close friend and his wife, Jim and Marie Mann, showed up that same weekend from Spokane. That cheered us both up, and we had an enjoyable time with them for a few days.

It was March 16, 1977, when we said aloha to beautiful Hawaii and to our friends, Sara and Dan Collins. They drove us to the airport and we promised to keep in touch.

Return to Spokane

Heather was shocked when she saw her dad. She said that she knew Phil had lost weight but she didn't realize just how much. We figured out later he had lost about 40 pounds in the short time since he first got sick. That in itself was a real cause for alarm. One doesn't lose that much weight without a cause.

Heather encouraged us to stay with her until Phil was feeling better. We had only been back a few days when we had to rush him to the nearest hospital. Obviously the breathing machine was not effective enough, and when I saw our family doctor making his early morning rounds, I asked him to take a look at Phil.

Our doctor told me right away that he would make the arrangements for Phil to see a chest specialist on that same day, March 21. We had to go across town to see this new doctor who specialized in immunology and pulmonary diseases. His name was Dr. Graves. When we arrived there, Phil was in very bad shape. He was given something right away for temporary relief. When the doctor was through checking him over, he told me he had given Phil an injection that would probably make him feel worse before he felt any better and indeed he did. We were to return in a few days for another examination.

During those few days, I could tell he was somewhat improved except for one thing. Phil was bothered again with his feet. This time it didn't stop there. The tingling went all up his legs and into his thighs. He was constantly rubbing them up and down. We thought he was just cold but when he started doing the same thing with his arms, Heather and I were quite concerned. When it was time to go back to Dr. Graves, I couldn't believe the change in Phil's asthma. He was like a new man. I think he thought that nothing short of a miracle had taken place. He could finally breathe, after all this time.

Of course the first thing on his mind now was getting back to work. I was hoping he wouldn't rush it. I thought he was being too hasty. It didn't take long for the Baker's Union to find out we were back home and one day they phoned to see if Phil was well enough to work at one of the supermarket bakeries. Easter was near and they needed extra help.

Dr. Graves gave Phil the OK so he went to work and got along very well. Just about a month to the day, he had to get another injection of kenalog. Again he perked up and was thanking the doctor for helping him feel well enough to keep on working.

He asked if there was anything he could do to show his appreciation and the doctor said that as a matter of fact, there was. His daughter was getting married in June, and he would like Phil to make the cake for the wedding. Phil said he would feel honored to do the job. We were invited to the wedding. Dr. Graves' daughter was a beautiful bride, and judging by the praises Phil received for the cake, there was no doubt he hadn't lost his artistic touch.

Phil stayed with this supermarket until after their usual Hawaiian Days promotion in July. At this time we made an effort to find a place of our own. We didn't want to impose on Heather's good nature any longer. We still couldn't find exactly what we wanted, but we ended up buying a mobile home. We thought that we would be able to move into the mobile home right away, but we found that it was almost impossible to find a space to rent. In other words, we had to wait for a vacancy in a park.

In the meantime, Phil was called on again to work at another supermarket. This time it was the Safeway Store at Manito Park on the South Hill. He started at the end of August. He would need another injection of kenalog before starting to work. It seemed as long as he was having these shots, he was able to keep going.

I asked Dr. Graves how often it was advisable to have these shots, and he made it clear that it wasn't advisable to have any at all but he added, we don't want him to choke to death. It was quite a while before I learned that kenalog is a steroid, but I still didn't realize how potent it was.

Toward the end of September, Phil was sent to be tested for allergies and he was found to be allergic to flour and all the grains. The allergy specialist advised him to have desensitizing shots which he did for more than two years. However, despite these shots and the kenalog treatments, Phil started having problems again and by late November he was forced to go on the sick list.

Early in December 1977, we got a phone call from a bakery owner in central California. He had read about Phil in a Northwest Bakers' Newsletter and tried to contact us several times. A friend of ours, Ronald Dunsmore, had mentioned Phil's name during an interview and the interview appeared in the newsletter.

When we first came to Spokane, we met Ronald Dunsmore. Once you saw this young man you never forgot him. He was a real character. Ron worked with Phil for a while but eventually went to work for his uncle who owned a bakery in Tillamook, Oregon. After he married his good looking wife Lois (a perfect match for him), they went into business themselves and wound up in The Dalles, Oregon. Being in the same business, we could empathize with any problems they encountered so we always kept in touch. They were very hard workers, and at the same time they managed to raise five children, four boys and one girl. Each one of them were just as crazy as their parents. I say this in a most complimenting way because they were so happy-go-lucky. They all did their share of work in the bakery and got a good college education. It is not surprising that they have all done extremely well for themselves.

Ron wanted to do cake decorating, but because he was left handed and Phil was right handed, it was difficult for Phil to teach him. Phil was determined to help him anyway and decided that, whenever we got the chance of a long weekend, we would drive to The Dalles and he would do his best to get Ron started. I enjoyed these trips as much as Phil did. There was always a few good home-cooked meals, and Lois was a great cook.

Phil's teaching extended to gingerbread houses for Christmas and a variety of novelties for Easter. After Ron became quite successful, especially with the wedding cake business, he was interviewed and the article appeared in the Northwest Bakers' Newsletter. It was at that time he made reference to the fact that he owed most of his success to Phil Richardson, owner of The Cake Box bakery in Spokane.

Some time later Ron took up painting for relaxation and the next time we saw them he offered us one of his works. That painting was a sailing ship at sea and became one of our proudest possessions.

In retrospect, this man in California (Bob Barker) was more or less like Ron but a much older man. His wife's name was Betty and, in time, the four of us would become good friends. He hadn't done much decorating and wanted to meet Phil. He explained there was a good cake decorating business to be had down where he was and he would like to add some of that to his current variety of bakery goods. He was disappointed to hear of Phil's sickness, but Phil told him if he got to feeling better we would try to go down to see him, if only out of courtesy.

At the beginning of March, 1978, Phil went to see Dr. Graves to get his OK to return to work and the doctor asked him what was the hurry. I was there and I remember Phil saying, "I do have to make a living."

The doctor replied, "You could go on public assistance."

To which Phil replied, "I do have my pride."

On the way home Phil was awfully quiet, and I questioned his silence. He said he felt as though he had just been insulted. He went on to say in an angry voice, "You know as well as I do, I've never been out of work in my life. I've never asked for a penny and I'm not about to now." I wasn't going to argue with him on that point, but I did remind him that Dr. Graves didn't know him as well as I did.

Phil got the OK to return to work. He had been receiving fifty dollars per week sick pay, but I know he would feel much better if he were getting his money the old fashioned way, by earning it.

Safeway Stores notified Phil that they were having a grand opening for their newly remodelled store in the Shadle Park area and they wanted to put him in charge of a cake decorating demonstration as part of their promotional attractions for one month. Phil would be working out front in the store so his picture was in their advertisements. They gave him quite a build up about his expertise on cake decorating.

Since this would not take place until mid May, we decided to go to the Social Security office to find out Phil's status on the amount he would be entitled to when he reached 65. We were advised to start drawing the Social Security immediately so that he could get retroactive payments as of age 62. Of course this would mean a small penalty of just a few dollars per month but the lump sum would certainly help us.

After the successful grand opening was over, Phil could have stayed on at the Safeway bakery in the bread and rolls department, but because it was now known that he was allergic to flour, Dr. Graves advised him against doing so. The doctor thought it would be OK to just go along with the cake decorating. However, due to the lack of available full-time work in that department, Phil's termination from the Safeway store came on August 1, 1978. At that same time he was asked if he would be willing to take part in future grand openings for any of their other stores and Phil told them he would be happy to do so whenever the occasion arose.

It was about this time I decided to discuss the Swine Flu affair with Dr. Graves. On Phil's next appointment I brought the subject up. I told him that when we were in Hawaii we had both had the shots on October 25, 1976, and that within 36 hours Phil got sick with flu-like symptoms. Dr. Graves thought it was very interesting and asked me if I had any kind of reaction at the time. I told him about the several episodes with my fingers and toes. I did have one more strange thing happen. One night I woke up with a numb sensation in my lower jaw. My tongue was so swollen I couldn't speak. I was horrified and thought I would choke. Luckily, with the help of my nurse friend Thelma, I got through the night and back to normal.

I considered that mild in comparison to Phil's problems so I asked Dr. Graves if he thought I might be able to apply to the government for some medical expenses. Many people were suing for damages, but Phil wouldn't hear of that. It would be silly of me to say the flu vaccine caused his asthma because he already had it, but never as bad. I thought because of his sickness and hospital bills in Hawaii plus work time loss, Phil should be reimbursed. Unfortunately, we left this until two years after the fact, and when I asked Dr. Graves if he would sign a form to help us he said there was little he could do because he hadn't known Phil prior to the incident in question. He said he thought I would have a better chance for a claim because of what happened to me.

I did get an attorney to draw up a form on which Dr. Graves stated that, in his opinion, the Swine Flu vaccine had triggered off a very severe asthma attack in Phil. Forms were also sent to the doctors who treated him in Hawaii and then to the government.

It was now very disturbing to Phil that he was limited in his choice of work, and he became very restless. We arranged to go to California but had to call it off because Phil did not feel up to the task. I was advised not to push him into any baking, but he set up his equipment in the mobile home and made an attempt to do the odd wedding cake. However, that was about all he could manage. Although I did all the preparatory work, it was clear to me he was having a terrible struggle. I would even have to finish some of the decorating myself. Maybe he was feeling unsure of himself. He was such a perfectionist, and a mistake could spell disaster for him. I hated to see him this way. This was not the Phil I knew.

For the next few months Phil's medical condition was up and down. He was still needing injections and inhalers. I was beginning to wonder if he would ever be well enough to work again. This is where the social security income came in handy. Combined with our savings, we were able to get by.

California

I think it was at the end of April, 1979 when we decided to make that courtesy trip to California because he was feeling somewhat better.

Cathy and Jeff just recently had their first baby, a boy named Chad Richards. They were both school teachers and lived in Kelso, Washington. They taught at Castle Rock High School. Cathy taught English and French and Jeff taught psychology, accounting, and other business subjects. He was also assistant coach in basketball, football and baseball so he was always kept busy.

We were anxious to see the new baby so we drove to Kelso first and then down the coastline to California. Bob and Betty Barker were happy and surprised to see us and insisted we stay at their home for a few days.

Their bakery was located in a small shopping center next to a supermarket, and being close to the ocean, they drew a terrific tourist business almost year round. A lot of this was in the early mornings from people camping out among the long stretch of beaches. They sold huge amounts of Danish sweet rolls, doughnuts, and other baked goods.

Phil wanted to pitch in right away but, much to his dismay, no matter wherever he was in the bakery it was almost impossible to avoid the flour dust.

We found the climate there was very moderate with little or no smog so we decided to stay for a while. Phil didn't altogether give up the idea of working, but since we were staying I was offered a job. I accepted only on the condition that we move into a small apartment close by. The cost of living was reasonable and besides, I kept hearing my dad's voice saying, "What will you do if Phil gets sick?"

Now, I could truthfully reply, "I will go to work for him."

Because of my experience, I was put in charge of the store and the young sales girls from 9:00 a.m. to 3:00 p.m. Betty and Bob worked long hours so they usually took a break during this time for about three hours. The show cases in the store were certainly not made for short people. I could barely see over the top. I was asked many times if I was standing in a hole. People often made comments to Phil about how short I was, but he always replied that I was short of nothing. I had never felt so conscious of my height, but I took it all in good spirit.

The bakery was closed Sundays and Mondays so Betty and Bob always made a point of having one of these days completely away from work and often invited us along. One time they took us down to Los Angeles to attend a Bakers' and Confectioners' exhibition which was a real treat.

We got along very well and they seemed to enjoy our company and valued our friendship. I think what they actually needed was for someone to come on a permanent basis, maybe a retired couple who could take over the business whenever they needed a break. We understood their need, but sad to say, although it would be an ideal setup for Phil and me, we couldn't give them any guarantee.

While we were in California, Phil would pick me up every day and then drive down the main street and straight on to the beach. We would then take off our shoes and walk for about half an hour along the edge of the water. It felt so good. Then we would sit in the car and watch the pelicans as they scooped up small fish. We also enjoyed seeing hundreds of seals sunning themselves on the huge rocks as the ocean swirled back and forth beneath them. On occasion, we were lucky enough to catch a glimpse of a whale spewing up a fountain of water or taking a giant leap in the mighty waves.

After the busy Labor Day was over, we went back home for a short while just to make sure the mobile home was OK and to visit with Heather and her family. Phil also got Dr. Graves to check him over and give him a kenalog injection.

After the moderate climate we had gotten used to, we didn't feel like facing another cold winter in Spokane. I was afraid if Phil had another asthma attack he could develop pneumonia, so I was as anxious as he was to get back to California.

By the time we got back, Betty and Bob had sold their bakery but were planning to buy another one, and in the meantime, they were working for the new owners until the end of the year. I was also asked to work at my usual hours because this was a busy time of year with Thanksgiving and Christmas coming.

Everything was going along nicely until one day something else hit Phil. We were in bed and about 2:00 a.m. I was awakened by what sounded like a slight moaning. I quickly turned on the bedside lamp, and I saw Phil's eyes roll back into his head. Then, all the blood drained from his face as his body stiffened and then went limp. I tried to get a pulse, but I couldn't. I was very scared until I saw the color returning to his face. Phil was not even aware of what had happened.

I went in search of a doctor the next day and was advised to make an appointment with a Dr. Drake. When he saw Phil, he was not able to shed any light on the incident. However, after a couple more of these same incidents he did call them syncopal episodes.

After the end of the year, Betty and Bob went in search of another bakery and wanted us to go along. Due to this latest development with Phil, I didn't feel that it would be a safe thing to do. The new owners, Mr. and Mrs. Clark offered to let me stay on with them and also to let Phil take a shot at some decorating.

It was only a couple of hours a day, but it was a real boost for his ego. It was at this time that our attorney notified us that our claim for medical expenses from the government was denied. Apparently the claim did not meet the necessary criteria, but we were allowed six months in which to appeal.

Our attorney told us he had discussed the matter with another attorney, but because of the thousands of dollars it would cost in fees, they would not recommend proceeding. He also pointed out that the medical report merely indicated there was a probability that the Swine Flu vaccine triggered off a severe asthma attack at that time. It did not relate that the Swine Flu vaccine significantly worsened the asthma, other than one single attack.

For the first time since Phil became sick, I saw him get upset. He wrote a letter back to our attorney saying that if we were in a better financial position, we would not hesitate to press the claim further but the expense prohibited further pursuance. Phil also said he was convinced that the vaccine not only caused the severe asthma attack in Hawaii which resulted in his being hospitalized for eleven days, but also other attacks when we returned to the mainland, not just a single attack. He also reminded our attorney that the doctors at the medical center in Hawaii had advised him to use (and sold him) a Maxi Mist breathing machine when he was discharged. This was in case he had another attack and could not reach a hospital so they evidently anticipated further attacks.

Phil was able to continue working the odd day once in a while, but in order to do so he needed the kenalog injections. He also had more of the syncopal episodes.

On June 23, 1980, early in the morning, he had a total of eight attacks in a period of six hours. Four of them happened in quick succession. After I phoned Mrs. Clark to tell her I wouldn't be in to work, I phoned Dr. Drake and he told me to get Phil to the emergency immediately. From there we were sent to the Sierra Hospital in San Louis Obispo. He was given all kinds of tests and when we got the results they showed that Phil had a calcification on the left side of his brain plus a seizure disorder. He was given seizure medication, dilantin and phenobarbital.

Now, he was faced with another dilemma. It would seem that not only had the Swine Flu vaccine triggered off severe asthma attacks, but it appears it may have opened up a veritable Pandora's Box. Was he now caught up in some kind of vicious circle where he was damned if he does and damned if he doesn't? The steroid which he had become dependent upon in order to breathe could possibly be the cause of the seizure disorder.

If there was anything good to report at this time it was when Mount St. Helens erupted in May, and we were lucky enough to be in California. Cathy and Jeff lived close to the mountain, and I was trying frantically to get in touch with them. When I finally reached them, Cathy said not to worry about them but be more concerned for Heather and her family. Ash was blowing fiercely away from the mountain and toward Spokane (over 300 miles away). The city was hit hard with the ash fallout and day turned to night because the ash completely blocked the sun.

This was such a terrible disaster. I said many silent prayers that my family were all safe. I was sure, had we been at home, Phil would not have survived the ordeal because of his condition.

About three weeks after Phil started the seizure medication I noticed a marked difference in him. I can only describe it as slight confusion, and the fact that he was repeating himself really bothered me. Mrs. Clark had also noticed a little strange behavior, too, so we thought it might be best if he quit work.

We stayed until August. I think it was about the second week when Phil had a bad day and he went to see Dr. Drake for the last time. The doctor told him then he may as well stop the desensitizing shots, apparently they had not been successful.

Before we said good-bye to our friends in California for good, we spent a few days repeating the simple pleasures we enjoyed down at the beach. When we got home, I made an appointment for Phil to see Dr. Graves sometime in September.

After we gave him all the information of the past several months, he wrote on his report that Phil now had a definite diagnosis of epilepsy. Unfortunately, the vicious circle was getting bigger.

The Circle Continues

By this time I was receiving my Social Security benefits, but our savings were getting very low. It wasn't long before many of our friends were asking why Phil wasn't working or back in business. They wanted to know what exactly was wrong with him. I explained his illness and the usual response was, "Why hadn't we tried to sue the government?" I repeated how Phil never wanted to sue but that we had applied to get some reimbursement for medical expenses and were turned down. I was told by a very concerned friend that since it was now obvious Phil's disease was insidious and he probably may never work again, it would be foolish of me not to file suit.

On our next visit with Dr. Graves, I told him I was concerned that Phil's confusion was getting worse. I asked him if it would be a good idea for Phil to see a neurologist and he said that would be a good thing to do. He made arrangements for us to see Dr. Best early in January, 1981. Dr. Best gave Phil a full neuro-evaluation and then we waited for the results of the C.A.T. scan and electroencephalogram (EEG).

Phil's memory was now impaired to the extent that I had to provide any information on his medical history. In return, the doctors would give me any instructions as to his medications. This meant that I had to go with Phil on any office call and be with him during evaluations. Phil seemed to take my word on everything and always looked at me with such trust in his eyes. I had the feeling that, as long as I was there, he felt safe and secure.

On our return, I reported to Dr. Best that Phil was having trouble again with the tingling in his arms and legs, but it didn't seem to register with him. He informed me that there was very little change in the tests in comparison to those taken in California. Dr. Best also added that there was nothing he could do about Phil's memory loss and that, probably, he was suffering from early senility. I could not, and would not, accept this diagnosis.

Heather said to me one day, "Why don't you take Daddy to a special clinic? Surely there has to be a doctor somewhere who can tell us what his real problem is."

I was sure I knew what his problem was. It's just that no doctor would agree with me or, if they did, they preferred not to get involved in what was slowly becoming a medical mystery. Heather and I both made inquiries and we came up with a clinic in Seattle. However, we couldn't take Phil right away because he was too sick.

It was still only January and there were days when the maximum expiratory flow rate of his lung capacity was as low as 90 liters per minute which was well below normal. It was at times like these when I watched him fighting for his breath. I felt so helpless. Why was he having these respiratory problems, and why was he having difficulty in swallowing?

I often thought to myself that, had Phil known how long he was going to be ill, he might have felt differently about suing the government. With that thought in mind, I decided to take off one day in search of a good attorney. I found one who turned out to be an excellent choice. The attorney's name was Gaither Kodis, and after I gave him all the details on Phil's problems, he seemed to be in total agreement with my feelings on the flu vaccines.

He said, "The government is a *tough nut to crack*, but since Phil had been tested positive for allergies to flour, he should be eligible for a disability pension."

Mr. Kodis then went on to ask, "Has Phil ever been told by any of his doctors that he has an occupational disease?"

I told him, "No, never."

He then explained, "In my opinion, Phil does have an occupational disease on the grounds of baker's lung. Therefore, it would make better sense to apply for the disability pension."

This sounded logical to me, and if Phil was legally entitled to it, I saw no reason why we shouldn't go for it.

Of course, it wasn't that easy. There was the matter of proving that baker's lung was indeed an occupational disease. Nevertheless, with the help of Dr. Graves, Mr. Kodis was successful in proving that fact.

Dr. Graves was called to the trial to testify on Phil's behalf. He agreed that, although Phil was found to be allergic to flour in September 1977, he had never been told he had an occupational disease until January 1981, at which time he was advised by Mr. Kodis to send in a claim.

I believe that, up to this point, Dr. Graves had been trying hard to solve Phil's respiratory problems and was not fully aware of the legal ramifications. It was a few years before the case was settled because it had to be determined who would be responsible for paying the pension. In Phil's case, the Department of Labor and Industries paid the larger portion and Safeway Stores paid a smaller percentage.

I was indeed, truly thankful for this. I dread to think of the consequences without their help. By the time we received it, I had borrowed 20,000 dollars from Phil's life insurance.

It was almost August before we finally got to the clinic to see the neurologist, Dr. Hardwick. Phil was admitted as an inpatient for a few days, and we got most of the results from the tests before we left. The doctor said there was definitely something very wrong with Phil, but he couldn't put his finger on it.

I asked him if he thought the Swine Flu vaccine was to blame and he replied, "No, it wouldn't be that."

He did give the following diagnosis: 1) There are no tumors. 2) The dilantin is wrong for him. The dosage was too high to which he added, "How the hell did this man tolerate it for more than a year?" 3) Phil is not "losing his marbles" and he pointed to the x-ray picture in question.

Dr. Hardwick then told me he would make out a prescription for a complete change of medication and see if he could get Phil back on the right track.

The next morning we were up and away for an early start back to Spokane. Cathy had recently given birth to a second baby boy. He was named Luke Clay. We were looking forward to seeing all of her family, even for only an overnight stay, so we went home by way of Kelso, Washington.

Phil wanted to take the scenic route through White Pass but it wasn't long before he started complaining about his right foot hurting him. We stopped several times and finally he took off his shoe to relieve the pressure.

When we reached Moses Lake, about 100 miles from home, he pulled into a rest stop. He looked ghastly. I thought he was going to pass out. I realized then that the numbing pain was interfering with his driving. He couldn't feel the gas pedal. I have always felt a sense of inadequacy for not being able to drive but never as much as I felt at this moment.

I was about to phone Heather for help when I saw this couple drive into the rest stop. I went over and explained our situation, and without any hesitation, they offered to help. They were going to Spokane to visit their son at Gonzaga University and the gentleman offered to drive our car while his wife followed in their own vehicle. By the time we arrived home, Phil was delirious.

The next morning the delirium was gone, but he was still experiencing the tingling pain in his foot. It was almost a week before he could walk normally again and the ordeal left him with a permanently crooked toe.

It was in the back of my mind that he was having the same kind of problem with his feet as he had experienced in Hawaii. The first time was right after he had the flu vaccines and then again when he was in the hospital. There had to be some connection between the two episodes.

On our return visit to the clinic six months later, there had been no improvement in Phil's condition. The new medication did nothing to control the syncope seizures. In fact, they were even more frequent. I would worry myself sick when he had several seizures in one day and wondered what affect they were having on his heart or his brain.

I knew I wouldn't be going back to Seattle again so I asked Dr. Graves to recommend another local neurologist for the purpose of regulating Phil's medication. He referred us to Dr. Houck and made an appointment for us to see him in July, 1982.

While we waited for our day to see Dr. Houck, we became involved with the activities of our grandchildren. Heather's three children were now in high school at St. George's, a private school noted for its excellent standard of education. This period of time turned out to be a godsend, not just for Phil, but for me also. Sandro, Simonetta and Cristina played on the basketball and soccer teams for the St. George's Dragons. Heather would pick us up on Friday afternoons, then drive us out to the school, which was on the far north side of town, to see these games. We would arrive early because Heather often took the stats for the games.

First, we would watch girl's basketball, then the boys and sometimes we saw the JV teams as well. Phil and I really enjoyed this because it was just the kind of diversion we needed. We got to know all the students, their parents and grandparents who came to cheer them on. After the games were over, we would all go to one of the students' home for a pot-luck party which was a lot of fun.

The weather wasn't always suitable for Phil to go to the soccer games but those we did see were great. After all, soccer being a British sport, was just our "cup of tea."

I have a special memory of those good times. Occasionally, there were sports awards banquets. On one particular night, Sandro seemed very insistent that Phil and I attend. Toward the end of the program, the Emcee proceeded to talk about a booster award being given this year to some special grandparents. I was stunned when he called out our names. I remember the students giving us such a rousing cheer. I thought they would raise the roof. I took Phil's hand and walked over to the award's table. I was so surprised I didn't know what to say.

I just said, "I feel like we have won an Oscar and forgot to write a speech." I did write a thank you letter to the school and ended by saying, "You don't have to take part in a sport to be a good one."

We received a beautiful plaque with our names inscribed on it. The thing that touched me the most was the emblem on the plaque which was a red, fire-snorting dragon with its lashing tail, featured on a white background (the school colors). Phil had drawn this emblem so many times on the top of large sheet cakes for this same school, even before our grandchildren were born. It seemed so fitting that this emblem was now being presented to us in a different form.

We kept our appointment, July 1982, with Dr. Houck. His first comment to us was, "Why did you come to see me? "You've already been to the best place in Washington."

From the moment he greeted us, in that cold and uninterested manner, I felt even shorter than short. I explained to him that I only needed his services to regulate Phil's medication and in case of any emergency that may arise from his seizure disorder.

The doctor told me that it would be necessary to do some testing first. I hated to put Phil through all this again so soon, but I didn't seem to have much choice so I told him to go ahead.

When we returned for the results, I thought I was better prepared than my first meeting with this doctor. He told us that he couldn't tell me anything different from previous evaluations except that Phil would not get any better and that he would continue to get worse.

I spoke up and said, "Can you possibly tell me if the kenalog injections might be the cause of Phil's seizure disorder?"

I knew that I was being intimidated when he responded with, "Lady, if you want to play doctor, don't come asking me questions, just stay home and save your money."

When I met with this kind of rude behaviour it made me think of the times I've heard advice given on television urging people to get a second opinion. "That has to be a lot of hogwash," I thought. I've been warned several times since that episode that my reputation will always precede me, no matter where I go. So much for second opinions. I had to let my skin get much thicker.

The next time we saw Dr. Graves I asked him, "What did Dr. Houck mean when he said that Phil was going to get worse?"

Dr. Graves replied, "He will probably lose his mind."

I looked straight back at him and said, "My God, when could this happen?"

He replied, "Tomorrow, the next day, a year from now."

By now I could hardly contain myself. I was shaking all over. I was thankful Phil didn't hear the conversation, but I knew he sensed something was wrong. This was just a preview of what was in store for me.

About ten days later I got the written reports from Dr. Houck which had also been sent to Dr. Graves. I read on the front page where it said: Diagnosis--dementia, probably idiopathic. I know now what that means but I didn't know at that time. I also know that ignorance breeds fear, but I didn't realize that it is almost imperative to have a degree in medicine in order to understand such reports.

In my ignorance, I came up with the notion that the word dementia meant demented and idiopathic, idiot. Therefore, when Dr. Graves told me Phil would probably lose his mind, my fear was now telling me that he eventually would become a demented idiot.

Is this what Dr. Houck's diagnosis really meant? How could this be when the doctor in Seattle had pointed out that Phil was not losing his marbles? Who am I supposed to believe? I was horrified! I put that report away without showing it to anyone, but I carried the burden of it around with me for years until I finally learned the true meaning.

What made this all the more atrocious was the fact that the report also stated that this diagnosis was discussed, at length, with the husband and wife and that, hopefully, that would help. It certainly would have helped a great deal if that were true but it was never discussed. Otherwise, how could I have been so devastated and lived in such fear. The only thing that man succeeded in doing was to intimidate and ridicule me.

Both our daughters were concerned about their father's illness. I'm sure it would cross their mind if he had something which may be hereditary. How could I possible show them that report? I know now that withholding the report from them was a bad idea. With their intelligence, they could have assured me and put my mind at rest, but my fear just got the better of me.

This episode was quite a setback for me. I tried to keep things as normal as possible, under the circumstances. I'm sure it was very frustrating for Phil at times. This was particularly true during his sick years because of the fact we were not able to make love anymore.

Of course this was due to the effects of all his medications, especially the steroids. I'm sure this abnormality would be very frustrating to any man. We could still love each other without the act of making love. Actions don't always speak louder than words. We kissed a lot and wrapped our arms around each other and always made sure we said, "I love you," before saying, "Goodnight." This way, I know he always felt that he was still loved. At least his memory impairment didn't change anything with respect to his sexual desires.

A Visit to England

I had been thinking a lot recently of how Phil should have the opportunity to visit family in England before he became too ill to appreciate it.

Phil's sister Edith had been trying to persuade us to go to England. I knew she would never come to the United States in that she had such a fear of flying. Her husband, Jack, owned and operated a successful butcher business so it was hard for him to get away. Anyway, knowing our financial status, they offered to help with expenses. Our family urged us to take this opportunity, so I finally agreed that we would take the trip.

Off we flew to England for 25 days in September, 1982. Edith and Jack drove to London to pick us up at Heathrow Airport. Phil hadn't seen them since we left in 1947. He hadn't seen his brother, Albert, either. Albert was also successful in the butcher business in the village of Barton-Under-Needwood.

I had always kept in close touch with Edith so she knew of Phil's illness. We had a wonderful time with them. They had a lovely home with a beautiful lawn, trees, and an abundance of flowers, especially roses. The garden was Jack's hobby. I felt like we were in a small park. It was very restful.

It happened to be our 45th wedding anniversary so Edith and Jack arranged a party for us. The party took place at a special inn called "Ye Olde Dog and Partridge," in Tutbury, Staffordshire. Legend has it that this 15th century inn was used by Robin Hood but it is more certain that Mary Queen of Scots was an occasional visitor during her happier visits to Tutbury Castle. When she was finally imprisoned at the castle, she reportedly was supplied with ale from this famous inn. This was the highlight of our trip.

Jack also drove us to the small village of Hanbury which was the site of the fatal bomb explosion in 1944. We went into the tiny church which survived the disaster and saw a large plaque with all the names of the victims engraved thereon. Phil remembered to point out the font made out of marble which came from the ill-fated marble pit and where he was baptized as a baby.

Before we left Staffordshire, Phil's brother Albert and his wife Iris gave a nice dinner for us at their home. We were able to meet all of their family.

The last part of our trip was spent with our friends, Dot and Joe Stenton. They lived not far from my family so it was easy to visit them at the same time.

Sad to say, this did not include my brother Walter. He died by taking his own life several years earlier. It is very hard for me to talk about it. The last time I saw him, 1957, he was so happy. I'm not able to pass judgment, I wasn't there. I was told he became heavily in debt because of his compulsive gambling. I only wish that those people who chose not to forgive him would understand, as I do, that compulsive gambling is just as much a disease as alcoholism. It is an addiction.

Phil and I both felt very bad and kept saying, "Had we have known, maybe we could have helped him." Regardless of the circumstances, I will never forget him. He was my brother and my friend.

I couldn't possibly leave Doncaster without taking Phil to see his baker friend of long ago, Les Emmerson. No matter whenever or wherever Phil's apprentice days in the baking trade were brought up, the conversation would always get around to Les Emmerson.

In his younger days, Les did have his eyes corrected and was now a fine looking man. He was married to an attractive lady. They were both saddened to hear about Phil's illness and when Les said to me, "Just fancy you came all the way from America and took time out to see me."

I replied, "Why not, you were his best friend."

P.E.T. Scan

It was in October of that year when my enthusiasm was renewed. I was always on the lookout for medical programs on television, especially those pertaining to the brain. Then one day I saw this show which came from Boston General Hospital and concentrated on a very sophisticated machine called Positron Emissions Tomography (P.E.T). They were demonstrating how this machine could pinpoint the most minute detail of the brain.

Watching this program gave me hope, and I immediately wrote to the hospital and told them about Phil's problems. I was pleasantly surprised to get a reply telling me they would be glad to see Phil in Boston. However, since winter was already upon us, it would be better for Phil to go somewhere like California. They urged me to press on and referred me to a medical center in Los Angeles and Dr. Charles Worthy, Professor of Neurology.

I wrote to Dr. Worthy and got an appointment to see him early in January, 1983. When our friend, Jim Mann, heard about this he offered to drive us to Los Angeles and make it a vacation for himself. Jim and his wife, Marie, had been our friends for many years. They moved from Canada about the same time as we did. Jim was on disability because of asthma and emphysema and could spare the time, so we took advantage of his offer.

Phil would now be able to sit back and enjoy the trip while Jim did the driving. It put a big smile on his face when we ran out of gas, of all places, on the San Francisco freeway. After three days on the road, we arrived in Los Angeles.

I liked Dr. Worthy from the moment we met. He asked if I was prepared to stay for a while so that Phil could be admitted into a special neurology clinic for a complete evaluation. This was fine with me, and since Phil was not altogether confined to the bed, we were able to walk around and get acquainted with this great medical center.

I often think of a funny incident that occurred in Phil's room. He shared a room with three younger men. One was a young man from China who was studying engineering. His name was Mr. Li. He had just been hooked up with an intravenous feeding tube and was told he must lay down and keep still for a while. It wasn't long before Mr. Li was up and seemed quite upset, so I went over to see if I could help him. He didn't speak very good English but I understood him when he kept repeating, "Too much bubbles, VELLY BAD, VELLY BAD. In China VELLY BAD, too much bubbles." He was very concerned about the amount of bubbles in the bag of liquid that was being fed to him through the IV tube.

I called for the nurse and at that moment Phil spoke up and said, "Don't worry, Mr. Li. The nurse made a mistake. She thought you were Lawrence Welk."

Of course, everyone in the room started laughing, except Mr. Li. I explained to him that Phil was a funny man. He looked at me seriously for a moment and then he said, "AAAH, FUNNY MAN, HA HA." Then he smiled so I knew he had caught on.

When Phil's sense of humor came through like this, on the spur of the moment, it was very encouraging to me. It told me he was still in my world.

I spoke with Dr. Worthy one morning and told him there had been a suggestion that Phil might have Alzheimer's disease. He said, "No, he doesn't have the countenance that goes along with the disease. What's more, he wouldn't be talking with such ease." He also said that I would probably be spoon feeding him or that he might even be bed-ridden by now if it was Alzheimers. The doctor said, "Most of the tests, so far, are inconclusive and I am afraid that Phil's brain damage is irreversible."

Regardless of the outcome, I was happy I made the decision to go to Los Angeles. I was very impressed with Dr. Worthy and with his efforts to leave "no stone unturned."

Three weeks later, I received the reports of the testing. There was the usual medical remarks, then the actual facts which came down to the following:

> No definite conclusion was reached as to the etiology of the different abnormalities observed.
>
> The patient had two lumbar punctures done, the first one showing clear colorless cerebrospinal fluid under normal pressure. The second one done thirteen days later showed the same, but with an elevated protein.
>
> A 24 hour cisternogram scan showed considerable reflux into the ventricles with minimum circulation compatible with hydrocephalus. The patient seems to have a communicating hydrocephalus which might benefit from neurosurgical intervention.

The next report mentioned several other possibilities but ended by saying that:

> Phil's problem is best defined as amnesia with memory disturbances complicated by frontal abnormalities, undoubtedly the effect of the left frontal mass lesion. Unfortunately, the cause of the amnesia is unclear and most known causes have been ruled out.

At least I could conclude that the brain damage seemed to be Phil's main problem. His asthma would appear secondary at this point. I knew that he had hydrocephalus, a condition which is characterized by enlargement of the cranium. This was caused by an abnormal accumulation of cerebrospinal fluid within the cerebral ventricular system, sometimes called water on the brain. It can also be caused by infection and tumors.

The Swine Flu is an infectious disease. There had to be a connection somewhere. According to the medical books, influenza is a viral infection of the respiratory tract. It was also a true fact that, after Phil had the two vaccines, I saw his asthmatic condition flare up almost to the point of "Status Asthmaticus", a medical emergency which can be fatal. I know that's what happened to him after several weeks of severe asthma attacks when he collapsed, and I had to call the paramedics in Hawaii.

I was getting so frustrated because I felt so sure I was right and most people agreed with me, except the medical profession. Yet, they were not able to tell me what was the cause of Phil's brain damage. Could it be that some of them had a slight suspicion I was right, but they didn't know what to do about the condition? Or, could it simply be that they knew the damage was already done and there was nothing they could do about it? Or, was it is much easier to define this mystery as Alzheimer's disease?

I was told more than once, so nonchalantly, to just take him home. They would say, "He's a happy man, he doesn't know."

I always replied, "He knows all right, what's going on, and so do I."

I had no one in the medical field to back me up so I didn't have a leg to stand on and felt like I was fighting a losing battle. Once again I could hear my dad saying, "Never let it be said that your mother bred a jibber." I must keep on trying.

I remember 1984 for many reasons, including persuading Phil to give up his driver's license. He reminded me that he never had an accident and only a couple of minor traffic violations. It was not that he was a bad driver, but he had great difficulty remembering which way to go or where he parked the car. I knew he was hurting. It was like another part of his manhood was taken away from him. I consoled him by saying it was better to quit while his record was still good.

It had been a year since our trip to Los Angeles and I wanted to go back for another evaluation on Phil. Our friend Jim wasn't available and I couldn't really afford for us to fly. I wrote to Dr. Worthy and asked if he could recommend a doctor in San Francisco who was on his level of expertise. I told him that we could go there on the bus, and we had friends (the O'Neils) we could stay with.

I soon got a reply from Dr. Worthy and a referral to see Dr. Erickson at a hospital in San Francisco. I made contact with the O'Neil Family in San Francisco and they were willing to help. Phil's x-rays were sent ahead, as requested, and we took off.

It was February, 1984. We got there on a Sunday and our appointment was for the Monday morning. By that same Monday afternoon I was ready to turn around and go right back home. I was in tears. I had hit another stone wall.

Dr. Erickson talked with Phil for a short while and then he looked over at me and said, "There is nothing I can do for your husband; he has Alzheimer's disease." He then stood up like he was about to leave and I noticed the x-rays on his desk.

I asked, What do you think about the x-rays?"

He shrugged his shoulders as he answered, "Oh, those don't do a thing for me." His voice sounded as though he resented my question. I had a feeling his mind was made up before he even saw us. Then he added, "I don't understand why Dr. Worthy hasn't told you this much himself."

My heart sank into my shoes as I went to the phone to call Maureen to pick us up. She persuaded me to stay at least until the next day. Phil gave me such a sad look as if he was more sorry for me than he was for himself.

I first met Maureen O'Neil back in 1960 when she came to our bakery to apply for work. We already had two efficient sales ladies who had worked for the previous owners, but when

Maureen came in the store that chilly morning, without any coat or sweater on, she looked as fresh as a daisy. She wore no make-up and her long, black hair was neatly arranged in a bun. Her rosy cheeks and deep, blue eyes were those of a true "Irish Colleen." I hired her on the spot.

Maureen's husband, Jim, worked in construction but business wasn't very good at the time. So, after a couple of years, they decided to take a chance in San Francisco. This was a smart move for them. They both worked very hard and became quite successful. Jim had a construction business of his own.

They never forgot Phil and me, and now, being the good friends they had always been, they advised me to phone Dr. Worthy in Los Angeles the next morning, which I did. After I told him about my brief encounter with Dr. Erickson, he said, "I have Phil's chart right in front of me and unless there has been a drastic change in the last year, he still does not have Alzheimer's disease." This certainly made me feel better, and needless to say, I didn't need any persuading to stay in San Francisco until the end of the week, as first planned.

The O'Neil's gave us the royal treatment. When I tried to thank them, they reminded me that I gave Maureen a job when she really needed one, and they were only too glad to help. They helped in many ways, but most of all, by making me laugh until I cried. I think this was about the last time that Phil projected any amount of reality. He related to their sense of humor, and this was certainly evident when Maureen reminded him of how he used to tease her in the bakery. This was usually about her strong Irish accent, but she took it all in the right spirit.

Maureen was devout Catholic and she never failed to pay for a mass to be said on religious holidays for Phil's recovery. With friends like these, our trip to San Francisco was not a complete loss after all.

M.R.I. Scan

Nineteen hundred eighty-four was also an exciting time for our Grandson Sandro. He won a $4000.00 scholarship to the university of his choice. This was offered every year by the Baker's Union Local 74 and all children of union members were eligible to compete for the award. It was a good start toward Sandro's four years at Western Washington University in Bellingham. That same year there was a lot of excitement about a special machine coming to Spokane, the Magnetic Resonance Imaging, or M.R.I. Scanner. A new building was being erected to house this machine right next to St. Luke's hospital.

"Come hell or high water," I was determined to get an M.R.I. scan for Phil. With this in mind, I searched for a good, local neurologist. This time I chose Dr. Roger Cooke and I made an appointment to take Phil to see him as soon as possible.

This doctor was a nice, soft-spoken person and seemed to be very understanding. He went through the usual routine of questioning Phil but he didn't do any extensive testing at this time. He thought that Phil's case was extremely complicated and doubted that anything would help him at this stage. Dr. Cooke suggested that I just bring Phil back at intervals to be checked over and to regulate his medication.

I asked, "Do you think that Phil might have, or maybe has had, the Guillain Barré Syndrome?" This was a disease which many people developed after having the Swine Flu vaccine.

He just said, "No."

I then asked, "What about the M.R.I. machine?"

He replied, "I don't think that would help either, but in any case, it won't be ready for clinical testing until the beginning of 1985."

In March of 1985, Dr. Cooke came through for us and Phil got the M.R.I scan. Some time later this was followed with a surgical correction employing a shunting technique as treatment for hydrocephalus. Although Phil came through the surgery fine, there was little or no improvement in his condition.

It goes without saying, I was very disappointed. This was getting to be like a broken record with the same thing over and over again. I was finding it harder to keep going but I just couldn't give up. We made four trips to Los Angeles, the last one in May, 1986. Jim Mann went with us.

My timing, I realized too late, was bad. Dr. Worthy was going on vacation in a few days, and because of this his work had piled up. To make matters worse, Phil had a seizure just before we left the hotel that morning. Consequently, I had a hard time keeping him awake and he was not very cooperative when the lady doctor was taking his vital signs. He kept pushing her hand away so I tried to explain his unusual behavior.

Phil was given a CAT scan and an EEG. Then he was finally able to get some sleep. It was 6:30 p.m. before we saw Dr. Worthy. He then apologized for being late. He took me aside, and to my surprise, he said, "I would have to conclude at this time that Phil may have Alzheimer's disease and that you should consider placing him in a nursing home."

I think this was the first time I ever lost control and cried in front of a doctor. At that moment I also lost faith, not only in the medical profession but also in human nature. I just couldn't believe my ears. I said, "There is no way I could ever do that."

To which he replied, "It would be better for you."

Then I really got upset. I said, "I haven't taken Phil to all of these medical centers just to make things better for me. The only thing that would make me feel better is if you or any other doctor can do something for Phil. He is sick and needs help, not me!"

When I saw Dr. Worthy the next day, I asked, "Is it possible to get a P.E.T. scan done on Phil?"

He said, "No, it is not possible, we don't do clinical tests here." He brought up the subject of the nursing home again saying, "It might be beneficial for Phil to go to a nursing home."

Again I was angry. I was still being haunted by the visions I had during the night of Phil being nursing home bound and in a wheel chair. I can only associate this vision with very old and very sick people. I know Phil was 72 but to me he had never been old. He had been ill for ten years up to this point but even at 62 we had only just begun to enjoy life at its fullest. It just wasn't fair.

I told Dr. Worthy, "I might consider taking Phil to some kind of senior center for possible stimulation, but I'm not promising anything." I suppose I shouldn't have gotten so angry, but at the same time I couldn't understand why the doctor had previously agreed with me on the subject of Alzheimer's disease and now suddenly he was doing a complete turn around. This was such a let down for me and very difficult to accept. I could not believe that Dr. Worthy came to this conclusion himself, and I wondered if someone else made the decision.

This was the second time I had been struck with fear, but now I knew that the best way to deal with the fear was to meet it head on and that's exactly what I did.

On the day that Phil was discharged, we went to the cafeteria before leaving the medical center. While we were having a little lunch, we did have a pleasant experience. I spotted a little lady in a wheel chair and I said to Phil, "I'm sure that's Grandma Walton from the Walton's TV show." He looked over and smiled as he nodded his head. We had always watched the show and I knew her real name was Ellen Corby. She had recently suffered a stroke. It seemed as though she was waiting for someone so we walked up to her just to say hello.

I said, "Aren't you Grandma Walton." She gave me the sweetest smile as she nodded her head. Then I asked how she was, and she just pointed to the wheel chair and then to her mouth. I took this as an indication she couldn't walk or talk as a result of the stroke, but she understood me, in spite of my Yorkshire accent. I then told this dear little lady how much we loved the show and hoped she would be able to return to it someday, which of course she did for a while.

I explained to her that Phil was sick with brain damage, and she looked at me sadly and then reached up and took his hand and placed it in mine. She patted our hands very gently.

I was in tears when we left her. The incident had brought back memories of my mother many years ago when I first showed her my tiny engagement ring. She made that exact gesture. I now felt a sense of peace for a little while and the next day we said our last good-bye to Los Angeles.

When the time came for our next visit with Dr. Cooke, I said to him, "I am very discouraged over our last trip to Los Angeles."

He told me again, "You have done everything humanly possible that anyone could do for their spouse. There is nothing else to do except a brain biopsy."

The Biopsy

In the meantime, Phil was becoming very withdrawn and making little or no conversation. We were getting to the point where we were like a couple of donkeys, just nodding.

I finally went to see the neurosurgeon, Dr. Mackay, and asked him to explain the procedure of a brain biopsy. He told me about the pros and cons and that it was possible Phil could die during the procedure, but on the other hand, he was physically strong.

He said, "You really don't have anything to lose, but there is a slim chance you have a little bit to gain."

Dr. Mackay had a very good reputation and he was the one who had done the shunt surgery for Phil. He said, "Think it over,"

My mind was already made up. I knew I could safely put Phil's life in his hands. I asked him, "Do you mind if I try once more to get Phil tested on the P.E.T. scan?" Somehow, from the first time I ever saw this machine on television, I had always thought it could work wonders.

Dr. Mackay was very understanding and said, "By all means, if that would give you peace of mind? Try for it and I will help you to get it."

There was a P.E.T. machine in Washington State but it was not yet in use so I chose to go to Irvine in California. We got a date set for October 24th, but I couldn't handle Phil alone on a plane so once again Jim Mann came to our rescue.

The test would cost $2,500.00 plus plane fare and expenses but that didn't bother me. I had to try it. I know Phil would have done the same for me.

We were interviewed by a very charming Oriental doctor and, after going through the preliminaries, he explained the procedures for the tests which took about three days. A special mask was made to fit Phil's face and when he was being placed on the P.E.T. machine, this doctor was extremely gentle .

I was told it would be close to three weeks before the results of this testing would be sent to Dr. Mackay. I finally heard from him and he told me to phone the doctor in Irvine because he wanted to speak to me personally. The first thing I was told was that this was not the scan of a person with Alzheimer's disease.

I quickly answered, "Thank God."

The doctor went on to say, "Phil has a slow growing, low-grade infection on his brain which could in some way be connected to the Swine Flu vaccine, but there is no way of proving that fact." Finally, he said, "I agree with Dr. MacKay that there is nothing to lose and you should go ahead with the brain biopsy."

It was certainly worth the expense just to get the negative on Alzheimer's disease and also for my peace of mind. Dr. MacKay was right about that much. Now all I could think about was the possibility of a small gain for Phil, so I went ahead and made all the arrangements for the surgery in January 1987.

After the Christmas holidays were over, I began to prepare myself for the most important decision I had made. Heather was concerned as to whether I could accept the consequences, whatever they might be, but I assured her I was prepared.

I don't consider myself a religious person, but I was no stranger to prayer, especially during the last ten years. At this time I was working overtime praying for the right answers.

When the day arrived, January 14th, I was there early so that I could see Phil before he went into surgery. The operation didn't take too long and when it was over Dr. MacKay and his partner came to tell me that Phil came through it very well and warned me not to get my hopes up too high. He also told me that the tissue that he had removed was diseased but not malignant. I was very relieved and thanked both of them for their good work.

As soon as I was told Phil was awake, I went into his room. He was still drowsy so I took his hand and stroked his face.

Suddenly he said, "You know, Jess, I've got a terrible headache today."

I was simply floored. Those were more words than he had spoken in weeks. I couldn't wait to tell the doctor. As the day wore on, he spoke several times, and when Heather and Ernesto came to see him, they were just as surprised as I was to find him so alert.

Before going home that night, I told Phil how good it was to hear him speak a full sentence after not talking for so long. He looked at me rather puzzled and said, "What do you mean I haven't been talking?"

I told him about his being so withdrawn and that he didn't even say his usual "Good Night" and "I Love You" anymore at bedtime.

He then raised himself up on his elbows and said, "But you do know I love you, don't you?"

"Yes, of course," I replied. I was so elated that I cried and went home feeling higher than a kite. It is impossible to describe my feelings, and no one could ever take that day away from me.

I got to the hospital early the next morning. Phil was propped up on his pillows but was sleeping, and in spite of his head being in bandages, he looked pretty good. I had just got settled in a chair at the foot of his bed when I heard a slight noise. I looked over at Phil just in time to see his head tilt back, and his eyes started to roll back into his head. At that very moment a young male nurse was passing by the open door, so I called out to him. I was sure this was exactly what happened when he would go into syncopal episodes (especially since they occur while he was sleeping). I had seen him have literally hundreds of them over the years.

However, Mark, saw the situation differently and he called out, "My God, get that code going." Quick as a flash, the code went out, "Code Blue, Code Blue!"

I ran from the room as a cart was rushed in and people both right and left were working on Phil. I was scared to death until I heard someone say, "I've got a pulse."

The doctor's offices were in the same building so they hurried over when they heard the code. Dr. MacKay assured me this had nothing to do with the surgery the day before, and Dr. Cooke didn't know what to think but he made the comment that he knew the medication, tegretol, affects the heart.

A cardiologist was brought in and I was told Phil would be fitted with a temporary pacemaker that day and then the next day it would be replaced by a permanent one.

Needless to say, I was a different person when I went home that night, but I tried not to let it get me down. At least Phil was still talking so all wasn't lost.

I was there the next morning for Phil's surgery, the third one in three days and again he came through with flying colors. He was kept in intensive care for a few days. I knew we would have to wait for the results of the biopsy, but in the meantime, I wrote a letter to the administration of the hospital.

I wanted to commend the young male nurse, Mark, for grasping the situation so quickly when Phil went into sinus arrest. He had evidently saved Phil's life, as far as I was concerned, and I wanted him to get the recognition he deserved.

At the same time, I was definitely concerned that if I was right and the arrest was the same thing I had witnessed all these years, had it finally caused enough damage to warrant the use of life saving techniques? If this was so, I couldn't help but wonder why Phil had not come to this point a long time ago and how on earth was he able to survive such a turmoil of traumatic events. If only I could get some answers. I was about stressed to the brink.

During Phil's week in the hospital, I was invited to a previewing of a brand new nursing home. This was attached to the hospital and was called St. Luke's Extended Care Center. I was encouraged to go in the event Phil was not well enough to go home. In that case, he would have been one of their first residents. I was impressed with the new facility and told myself that if Phil did get to the point where I couldn't handle him (heaven forbid) then this was the place I would choose.

After he was home he did improve somewhat but only by way of communicating a little better and if this was the little gain I had hoped for, I was extremely thankful. All medication was stopped and Phil did appear a little more alert.

The Nursing Home Decision

This was the year of our 50th wedding anniversary and we had always promised ourselves we would go back to England and renew our vows in the church where we were married. I asked Dr. MacKay if it would be safe for Phil to make the trip. He thought it was a great idea and told me to go ahead and have a good time.

Heather had been working in the library at Gonzaga Preparatory School for a few years but had recently given up the job to help me in caring for Phil. This was the second time she came to our rescue. The first time was after she graduated from North Central High School. She then went on to college but cut her college short when she knew we were in desperate need of help in the new bakery business. I thought it would be nice for her to go with us on this trip.

Cathy was now teaching French at Kelso High School and she had helped her students with fund raising projects to help them make trips to France. She was going with them again this year and Jeff would stay home with their two boys.

We all agreed it would be a good idea to wait until Cathy got back and then Jeff could go to England with us. He had never been outside of the U.S. so he was looking forward to the adventure. Heather and I would be glad of his help with Phil, especially on the plane.

I wasn't sure that Phil could handle the excitement of a wedding anniversary party so I didn't plan one and besides we were there a little ahead of the anniversary date. Anyway, we were at least able to attend a Sunday service at St. James Church and to meet a few old acquaintances, after which, we strolled through the village. We stopped to take pictures in front of the two small cottages which at one time had been home to us. The village itself had changed very little but the outskirts were all built up almost beyond recognition.

We soon found out that Phil wasn't comfortable in large crowds. In planning events, we made sure that one of us would be able to stay behind with him. Phil was content just to visit with his sister Edith and her husband Jack. The same was true when we stayed with our friends Dot and Joe Stenton. He liked to be around Joe and take short trips to the coast. Jack, Joe, and Jeff were able to take care of Phil's grooming. He had no qualms over that, and it made things easier for me and Heather.

During our stay, Heather was able to fly over to Belgium to visit with friends. She also went with Jeff to see the beautiful country in Wales. We were all able to go to the city of York where stood the famous York Ministry which had been badly damaged by fire, but recently been restored to its former splendor and architectural beauty. This was, without a doubt, a wonderful sight to behold. We also walked through the narrow streets paved with cobblestones and the many market places and shambles which are a different kind of tourist attraction.

Before we left England, my sister Elsie and her two daughters, Betty and Pauline, arranged a family reunion for us which was a very pleasant surprise. Betty's husband, Malcolm Dean, was an excellent host and gave us a special toast (though a little early) for our 50th anniversary.

I think I can speak for the four of us when I say a good time was had by all. And no, we did not go to see the Queen because as Phil would have said, "Why should we? She never comes to see us."

I was also happy we took this trip because it turned out to be the last time we saw Phil's brother-in-law, Jack Wright. Not too long after our visit, Jack died suddenly from a heart attack. Phil's sister, Edith, now lives alone, but I have kept in close contact with her.

It was now August 28, and we had been back from England about a month. We had just finished breakfast one morning, and Phil was in his chair watching television while I went about my daily routine.

Suddenly I heard this funny sound. I thought it was from the TV, but then something struck me and I ran into the living room. I could see right away that Phil's hands were gripping the arms of his chair while, at the same time, he was pressing his back against the back of the chair with all his strength. I thought it would tip over.

He was making this terrible, loud, shrieking noise. It sounded like, "EEEKA, EEEKA, EEEKA." It went on continuously, forced through his clenched teeth. His face was very distorted and his eyes were blinking non-stop. It was like he was in great fear that some kind of raging monster was attacking him.

I stood there helpless, thinking he was going to die of fright, any moment, right before my eyes. I was sure this was the end. After what seemed an eternity, the shrieking stopped, but then he started thrashing around. He was flinging his arms in every direction. My intuition told me this was definitely a Grand Mal epileptic seizure. I had to wait until he stopped and his body went limp before I could run to the phone. I called 911 first and then Heather. The paramedics were at the door in five minutes and Heather was close behind.

This whole thing lasted about 15 minutes, but Phil had still not come around when the help arrived. They first asked about the dosage of dilantin he was taking? I told them, "He hasn't had any seizure medication since January." I also made it very clear that dilantin was wrong for him and that he had taken tegretol for six years prior to last January. They called for an ambulance to take Phil to the emergency at St. Luke's Hospital. Heather followed behind us.

After waiting approximately half an hour, we were told he would have to be admitted to the hospital. Before I went to the office to give all the information, I wanted to take a peek at Phil so they allowed me to go into his room. I asked him, "Are you OK? Do you know your name?"

He nodded yes to both questions.

I noticed the nurse was injecting him with something so I asked, "Is that dilantin?"

She replied, "Yes, and because of the amount it has to be injected very slowly."

I got very upset when she said that. I asked, "Did the paramedics explain about Phil's situation and his previous problems with dilantin?"

She said, "It is up to the emergency doctor to decide and they always give dilantin to seizure patients because it's a stabilizing drug." Then she added, "It's not going to hurt him."

When they got Phil fixed up in his room, he went into a deep sleep, and by now I was exhausted so I tried to take a nap. Some time later they took him for a C.A.T. scan, and after that they found he had injured his tail bone, possibly while he was thrashing around during the seizure. This was causing him a lot of pain.

I went home that night feeling very depressed. What next was going to happen to him? It all seemed so unjustly cruel for him to suffer this long. I was tempted (momentarily) that night to pray for him to die, but I couldn't do it. I loved this man with all my heart and soul. I had to keep on trying.

The next day when I got to the hospital I had to face another dilemma. If it hadn't been serious it would have been funny. Phil was wide awake and talking a blue steak. He couldn't stop laughing and was constantly reaching to grab things in the air that weren't there. Then he tried to thread a needle, even to the point of wetting the thread (supposedly in his fingers) to get it through the eye of the needle. Worse yet, he didn't even know me for a while.

All the nurses knew him from when he was there in January and were very kind to him, but they had never seen him act this way before. They thought the same as I did, that it was the affects of the dilantin (so much for the stabilizing drug). Although his old chart had listed tegretol as his medication, they had to follow orders from the emergency doctor who admitted him because Dr. Cooke was off that weekend. Of course this meant continuing with the dilantin until Monday.

Phil's behavior was not so weird as over the weekend, but I was surprised when they told me he could go home on Tuesday. I was a little apprehensive as to whether I would be able to handle him and told the nurse about my doubts. I was hoping there would be no problems.

The first day he was home was OK until during the night. I felt him stirring around in bed, as usual, in his effort to get up to go to the bathroom. I immediately walked around to help him, but before I could reach him he fell out of bed. This was one of many bad nights to come. I struggled for more than an hour trying to get him on his feet and ended up dragging him by the ankles as far as the bathroom. Every movement he made was so painful for him, but I finally got him back to bed. I knew it would take time for Phil to recover from this kind of stupor, which evidently was brought on by the drugs, but I didn't think I could handle it through another night.

I remembered that when I went to view the nursing home I had put Phil's name down just as a precaution so now I decided to phone and ask if I could take him there temporarily until he was back to what was normal for him. They refused me saying there were no empty beds. I was very disappointed and even more so after we both went through untold agonies for two weeks.

I found out later that there actually were empty beds. I was told that their had been an oversight and that Phil's name was not on their list.

Although he survived this latest ordeal, he continued to have Grand Mal seizures about once a month and in spite of being put back on medication they were never under control. Thank goodness they were less severe than the first one, but he was never the same after that horrible experience. It really took its toll on him, slow but sure he began to lose the ground he had gained after the brain biopsy.

The circle definitely got more vicious than I could ever imagine. I remember thinking, "What on earth am I going to do now?" It was at times like these I asked myself, "Why is this happening to us and what did we do to deserve this?"

We both had made mistakes and we had our rough times, but who doesn't? However, we were always able to overcome anything that would have affected our marriage in a negative way. I think the more than 50 years is proof of that. As I looked at Phil and saw how totally dependent he was on me, there was no other place I would have rather been than by his side. I would have given my right arm to release him from whatever it was that held him hostage in his own body. I just could not let him down.

When Phil got his disability pension, he was still able to communicate with me. He made me understand enough to be sure and pay off the money I had borrowed from his life insurance. We also sold our mobile home and moved into a nice new apartment on the ground floor with all the many modern conveniences. This was better for us because by now (Spring 1988) he was not capable of doing any maintenance of any kind. I got someone from an agency to come to the apartment to bathe him. I could still manage to cut his hair and shave him but I had to turn into a contortionist to even manage that much. We just lived a quiet life. We watched a lot of television and continued our daily walks. I was always trying for something to stimulate his life.

One day I told Dr. Mackay how much Phil enjoyed swimming so he agreed to sign a form which would allow him to go to the YWCA twice a week. It had been ten years since he did any swimming so I wondered if he still knew how. There was no need to worry. As soon as he hit that water, he took off like a tadpole and a volunteer had to go after him.

Everyone made a point of telling me that Phil was indeed a strong swimmer and it did my heart good to see how well he performed, considering all he had gone through. I think for a short time he felt like he had been let loose.

However, each time I took him it became more difficult for me to handle him. There was something strange going on. It had something to do with getting him dressed and undressed. I have always tried to protect his privacy but it seemed like he was going through a new stage. This was happening during the night also. Whenever he went to the bathroom, I would go after him but there was no way he was going to let me pull down his underwear. It was becoming a regular struggle and I would end up having to forcibly push him down on the toilet while he hung on to my arms. After a while, my arms would bruise from the strength of his hands as they clung to me. I would get angry and say things like, "Why are you doing this to me," as I showed him the bruises.

He always looked at me with such anguish in his eyes and that look would haunt me (and still does). I could feel his eyes following me everywhere as though he was pleading for answers I couldn't give him. I would panic sometimes at the thought of him dying and this would make me even more angry. Then I would take my anger out on him. I would ask myself, "How could I treat him this way and why do we always hurt the ones we love most?" My guilt was overwhelming but so was my grief. Many times I would hide in the bedroom where I would cry an ocean of tears.

No matter what happened, he always seemed relieved when I put my arms around him and told him how sorry I was. His eyes took on a different look as if to say, "Don't worry, Jess, it's OK."

The summer swimming was over. Dr. Graves was retiring soon and we would have to get someone to replace him. Nineteen eighty-nine was a mixture of emotions for me. Phil continued to have Grand Mal seizures and would appear stubborn at times.

Heather wondered if he needed new glasses. She noticed he was having difficulty getting in and out of her Volkswagen bus and seemed very unsure of his footing.

Quite by accident, I heard about a therapy class being offered by Eastern Washington University (EWU). This was at its downtown Spokane center for the speech and hearing impaired. I took Phil to this center for an evaluation and was told he was aphasic and it was doubtful the therapy would help. On the other hand, it might stimulate him and we were welcome to attend. This appealed to me right away, and I think it was March when we started. I realized this was one of the best things I did for Phil.

Although he rarely spoke, like most of the male class members there, he could sense the funny side of a sad situation. Some of them were stroke victims and were so intent on trying to get a word out that they would almost turn blue in the face and that's where the fun came in. They would laugh with each other over their frustrations and with the young therapists who, I thought, did a remarkable job. I think the therapists, both male and female, were students doing graduate school work.

When I looked up the word aphasic in the dictionary it said: A total or partial loss of power to use or understand words, usually caused by brain damage or injury. This was another interesting clue, at least for Phil's speech problem, so that when one of the teachers suggested I take him to a certain psychologist, I didn't hesitate.

Dr. Robert Attwood worked with some of the people who attended the therapy classes and also taught psychology at EWU. He had an office downtown and this is where we met him. This doctor explained a lot to me about Phil's behavior, especially the bathroom problem. He said, "In a man's case, he resents receiving too much assistance from his wife because of the fear of losing dignity." He went on to say, "Phil has aphasia and he is very insecure about a lot of things so he needs a lot of understanding."

He advised me to buy an armchair commode with a seat belt. This way he could feel the arms as he sat down then I could fasten the seat belt and leave him to his privacy, as long as necessary. I did this and it helped a lot. It made sense to me. I don't know why I didn't think of it myself. But then, why should I berate myself? I should be asking, "Why hadn't any doctor detected the aphasia before now?" Maybe they did and, if so, they just failed to tell me. This was a step in the right direction for me, thanks to EWU.

When Cathy and Jeff came for their usual summer visit, they took care of Phil so that Heather and I could have a little respite. It was easy for Jeff to lift him in and out of the bath tub and do the rest of his grooming.

As time went by, I knew the situation was getting more difficult for me. When Heather brought up the subject of a nursing home I didn't like it, but I knew she was right. Sometime later I went to St. Luke's Extended Care Center to tell them of my decision to take Phil there and because he was high on their list we only had to wait approximately two weeks.

During those two weeks I happened to see a television special about seizures from the heart and from the brain. I could remember one doctor's name and that he was at Scripp's Research Clinic in California so I wrote him. I was determined not to let Phil go to a nursing home without one last fight.

As soon as Dr. Gregory Del Zoppo received my letter, he phoned me and said, "Lady, I know you need help." This doctor's phone call helped restore my faith in the medical profession. He told me to contact a colleague of his who was also on the same TV show. His name was Dr. Bruce M Coull. He was an Associate Professor of Neurology at Oregon Health Sciences University in Portland, Oregon. I wrote to Dr. Coull right away and received a phone call from his office telling me he would see Phil as soon as possible. I would be notified by mail.

It was the saddest day of my life when I took Phil to St. Luke's Extended Care Center on November 16, 1989. To add to my torment, I was forced to apply for Medicaid assistance. Our total income, including Phil's disability pension, was not enough to pay the nursing home so I had no choice. I went to the office to give all the information while Heather got him settled in his room. I stayed at the nursing home quite a while to observe the routine and meal times.

I think Phil sensed he was among friends. After the evening meal, which he ate with gusto, he was prepared for bed. When I saw he was comfortable, I went home to my empty apartment. I have never cried with such despair. I felt terrible and couldn't sleep for thinking about him.

Day two. To my pleasant surprise, Phil appeared to be settled in. His eyes lit up when he saw me. I could tell he was enjoying all the attention showered on him as a new resident. Again I stayed most of the day, and when I saw the meals that were given to these residents, it was plain to see they were very well fed. It only took a few days to realize I had done the right thing in bringing Phil here. Not only was the whole staff good to him, but they were very kind to me too. I could now rest a little easier.

I was soon to become a member of this big family. I took two buses to get there almost every day, and Heather would go on week-ends to give me a break. Phil was always waiting for me with his usual, "Hey!" This was about all he could say, but it was enough to let me know he was glad I was there.

It was easy to get hooked on some of those residents at St. Luke's. The little lady who sat on Phil's left in the dining room was ninety-nine years old. She reminded me of Phil's little old granny with her small eyes sunk in her head but she could read without glasses and had the sweetest disposition. I shared Phil's treats with her and she would exclaim, "Oh goody," and "Thank you, honey."

Seated on Phil's right was his room-mate, a real happy-go-lucky individual. His name was Joe Golik. Joe had been a barber at one time and he loved to sing. I always wished that Phil could have conversed with him, but I think somehow they had their own way of communicating.

During Phil's first week we were introduced to a lady as one of our countrymen. Her name was Doris Nelson. She told me she came from Middlesbrough in Yorkshire. My father would have described Doris as a "real genteel lady." She had beautiful silver-grey hair and a real peaches and cream complexion. I soon became very close to this pretty lady and would visit with her often just to reminisce about home.

We were both in agreement about the thing we missed most which was the English food. Doris would say, in her Yorkshire accent, "EEEE, Jessie, I would give anything for some good fish and chips or a piece of Melton Mowbray pork pie!"

I was mostly impressed by how much she could remember at age ninety-three. She could remember buying meat from the Schumm brothers. They were the gentlemen who my mother provided with bed and breakfast during the Doncaster St. Leger race week more than 50 years ago. Doris told me there were several brothers and they had a good butcher business. This is indeed a "small world" after all.

I was not the only one, by any means, who made daily visits to St. Luke's. There were many caring people that came to see a spouse or parents. I got acquainted with many of these people and particularly with an elderly couple named Bessie and Otto Mehew. They reminded me so much of Phil and me. Otto was always clowning around and Bessie, a tiny person like me, was always going along with his jovial personality. To me these two people, who visited with their daughter every day (she was stricken with M.S. years earlier), resembled a tower a strength. I felt privileged to know them.

Confirmation

By the end of the year, I received word that I could take Phil for an appointment with Dr. Coull on January 12, 1990. Our first meeting with him was very pleasant. He shook hands with Phil and said, "Hello Phil, I'm Dr. Coull."

Much to my surprise, Phil gave a chuckle and said, "Oh yeah."

Dr. Coull shot right back and said, "I'm not that cool, Phil. I don't spell it that way."

Phil was still smiling when he was taken to be examined so I knew he felt comfortable with this doctor. When they returned the first thing I was told was that there was nothing wrong with his heart. Dr. Coull continued by saying that it was conceivable that Phil has had post-infectious encephalitis of the brain (which is lethal). This was after viewing the x-ray pictures I had taken with me.

He said, "The ventricles are swollen and perhaps had leaked. There is a possibility this was caused by Swine Flu vaccine, but it would be very hard to prove it." He also added, "I'm sorry to tell you that it's too late to sue the government." Dr. Coull also thought Phil may have had Guillain Barré Syndrome.

I asked, "Did the kenalog injections, which Phil had to take all those years to relieve his asthma, have some bearing on his present condition."

The doctor said, "It probably relieved his asthma, but it didn't do anything for his immune system." He hastened to say, "The real culprit was the vaccine."

I knew then that my search was over and the word "lethal" said it all. At least, I knew my suspicions were right all along and someone was actually on my side. Finally Dr. Coull confirmed what the psychologist had told me about aphasia and more so. He pointed out how Phil looked only to his right and veered off to his right side when walking which was a frequent problem of patients with aphasia.

After I got Phil settled back into St. Luke's, I took part in all kinds of activities with him. I felt it was better to do this than stay home alone. I often took tapes of old time sing-a-long tunes so that the other residents could join in and have a little fun. I would also take some nice dance music in the hopes I could get Phil to try dancing. I was lucky if he was able to even stand up and I would end up going through the motions and sway to the music alone. I often saw a tear in his eyes as he bent down to give me a kiss.

He was already becoming more and more insecure. His swimming days were now over because I refused to give him seizure medication. The staff at St. Luke's didn't want to be responsible in case he had a seizure in the pool, which I understood.

Heather and I couldn't see any sense in visiting with Phil every day if he was drugged to the point where he didn't know us. Even at the risk of having seizures, we would rather he had quality time and stay alert. We had that choice and most of the nurses were behind us one-hundred percent.

It was now becoming obvious that Phil's vision was impaired, as Heather had suspected a long time ago. He was so insecure and walking so slow like every step was a great effort so I bought him a wheel chair.

It seemed strange to a lot of the staff that Phil had lost almost all the power of doing anything for himself. He knew what he wanted to do, but he couldn't do it. He knew what he wanted to say, but he couldn't say it.

Even though he was very inactive, he still had such strength in his hands. I would explain that his strength came from carrying hundreds of wedding cakes over the years. It was not just the weight of the four or five tier cakes but holding them at arms length so as not to ruin the delicate work. He would carry them out of the bakery, into the station wagon, back out of the wagon and up and down church steps. The aides could feel this strength when he hung on to them, just as I had felt it so many times before.

Now I was having to feed him because even all that strength couldn't direct his food to his mouth. At least his appetite remained good.

From what I read, it is important to realize that for all these inabilities there is not necessarily a loss of mental competence. This much I have been aware of all along because Phil was always able to convey to us that his sense of humor was still there. However, now the only way he could project his humor was with a wink, a smile, or a shake of his head.

I would wheel him around and we would visit with many residents who often turned out to be old customers of ours from when we had the bakery. I volunteered to work in the gift shop, and Phil was allowed to be there with me in his wheel chair. I got to know many visitors who came in to buy gifts, especially around Christmas time. This was when the lady in charge of arts and crafts, Joann Chandler, always came up with a wonderful display. Many small items were made by the residents under her skillful care.

The Circle Grows

Cathy and Jeff went with me to Portland for another consultation with Dr. Coull. He made a point of telling them that Phil did not have alzheimer's disease and he never did have it. Sometime later, he sent me a report along with an article which he and his colleagues had written entitled--Multiple Cerebral Infarctions and Dementia Associated with Anticardiolipin Antibodies (ACA). This article also included a number of clinical manifestations of Anticardiolipin Antibody Syndrome. I found several that were compatible to Phil's many problems. Dr. Coull wrote in his report:

> I think that we have pinned down at least the source of your husband's problem to be related to the presence of ACA. We have found these antibodies in a number of patients who have experienced multiple strokes and disability because of altercations in memory and impairments of language and thinking. We can say, without a doubt, that this problem is related to the immune system and the production of antibodies which somehow trigger the coagulation process. We don't know for certain why people develop these antibodies. Your recognition that Mr. Richardson's problem began shortly after a Swine Flu inoculation is an interesting clue. As I have mentioned before, people have had immunologic nervous system problems after Swine Flu vaccination. The relationship between ACA's and Swine Flu vaccine is not established or explored so that I cannot confirm this linkage

> in your husband's case, but it certainly is a possibility and my colleagues and I will discuss this.

As soon as I received this report, in January 1991, I decided to do a little research myself by going to the Eastern Washington University library. It was there where I met a young lady librarian by the name of Cindy Miller. When I told her that I was interested in any articles on the Swine Flu and the Guillain Barré Syndrome, she proved to be a big help to me. She was a real eager beaver.

Cindy found me another article on Anticardiolipin Antibodies similar to the one written by Dr. Coull and his colleagues. This one, by Steven R. Levine, MD and KMA Welch, MD, was written a little later. One thing I read in this article which I considered interesting was the fact that the two doctors included in their clinical manifestations of ACA's the Guillain Barré Syndrome.

Eventually, I purchased a book entitled, "Pure Politics and Impure Science, The Swine Flu Affair." This was written by Arthur M. Silverstein, a Professor of Opthalmic Immunology at the John's Hopkins University School of Medicine and published by the Johns Hopkins University Press. I now had a veritable fountain of information at my service. This book was very revealing, especially to me, and it didn't take long to realize that the National Influenza Immunization Program turned into a real fiasco.

I also read that, without an appreciation of both the history and science of influenza, it would not be possible to understand why the Swine Flu Affair of 1976 unfolded as it did. According to Professor Arthur Silverstein, the aftermath of the Swine Flu fiasco saw two of the nation's highest ranking public health officers dismissed. Professor Silverstein, however, felt that the true villains of the episode were the Swine Flu itself which, with characteristic fickleness, failed to reappear; Legionnaires Disease, an unrelated but baffling ailment did appear causing a panic that revived the dying swine flu program; Guillain Barré Syndrome, the crippling and potentially fatal side effect of swine flu vaccine, which assured the program's reputation as a disaster; and finally the political priorities that were allowed to control so many crucial decisions. One thing that puzzled me was, with so many high ranking officials in this enormous task, why did it appear there was such a great lack of leadership?

There were many obstacles which seemed to plague the program. One important problem was the matter of insurance. Silverstein states:

> Throughout the period (April and May) the insurance industry continued its pressure on the government to take them off the liability hook, primarily by threatening to terminate the insurance coverage of the manufacturers. Without insurance, the manufacturers would refuse to release the vaccine and the entire program would flounder.

There was also the problem of the informed consent forms (Chapter Eleven). Evidently, some 60 million printed forms dated July 15, 1976 had already been distributed. These were of two types. One was for use with the monovalent swine flu vaccine and the other for use with the bivalent vaccine (A/swine + A/Victoria). The forms indicated that the vaccine would protect most people from swine flu during the next flu season and that it could be taken safely during pregnancy and that most people have no side effects from the vaccine.

The forms went on to advise that tenderness at the sight of the shot may occur and last for several days. Other side affects were fever, chills, headaches, or muscle aches within the first 48 hours. As with any vaccine or drug, the possibility of severe or potentially fatal reactions existed. However, flu vaccine had rarely been associated with severe or fatal reactions.

My husband experienced all of the possible symptoms within the first two days following the vaccinations, only they didn't stop there. He developed one thing after another and had to be hospitalized.

A great amount of controversy arose over these forms. They were faulted for not having pointed out more clearly the risk of neurologic and other disorders that had occasionally been reported in the past to follow almost any type of vaccinations. In addition, there were vaccine production problems in that there had been the use of a wrong seed virus. Had we known all of this back in October of 1976, I doubt that we would have agreed to take the vaccine. We had seen President Ford taking the vaccine on television which was enough to persuade us it was the right thing to do, and we signed the forms in good faith. However, we never saw even a hint of adverse reactions on the forms so dangerous as Post Infectious Encephalitis of the brain, Hydrocephalus, Guillain Barré Syndrome, and Aphasia. There was also the possibility of other irritating things such as adverse reactions to medications which caused convulsive type seizures, then epileptic Grand Mal seizures.

One thing I didn't understand and would certainly have appreciated an explanation for is that if the vaccines were named monovalent for the Swine Flu vaccine alone and bivalent for the Swine Flu vaccine combined with the A/Victoria flu vaccine; why was my husband given both the bivalent and the monovalent at the same time? Should not the bivalent have been enough and were those people who injected the vaccines at the various health centers not experienced enough to know that such an amount was definitely in excess?

Phil told me that, because of his asthma, he was advised to have two injections and was given two forms to sign; one blue and one white. Did the person who gave him the shots make a mistake or was that person not enlightened enough to do the job properly? Whatever the explanation, when he received those vaccines, which were given by jet guns, presumably to speed up the process; they might just as well have put a real gun to his head right there. As Dr. Coull had said, "It was his opinion that the vaccine was the real culprit and Phil never had a chance."

I made a point of studying Guillain Barré Syndrome mainly because Dr. Coull thought Phil may have had the disease early on. It certainly was no surprise to find that most of the symptoms of the disease related to Phil's condition. It would seem my suspicions were justified about the connection when his feet and legs were bothering him and also when he couldn't eat because he was so short of breath thus making it difficult for him to swallow. Another excerpt from Silverstein's book seems to prove my point when he writes:

> The disease usually begins with a tingling in the extremities and weakens the muscles. This is due to damage in the peripheral nerves in the arms and legs which may ascend rapidly, and involve the central nerves that control breathing and swallowing.

Finally, I bought the medical book entitled, "Encyclopedia and Dictionary of Medicine, Nursing, and Allied Health," by the late Benjamin F. Miller, MD. and the Claire Brackman Keane, RN, BS, MED, published by W.B. Saunders Company. An excerpt from this book, which proved to be invaluable to me in many instances, explained the Guillain Barré Syndrome as follows:

> A relatively rare disease affecting the peripheral nervous system, especially the spinal nerves but also the cranial nerves. Pathologic changes include demyelination, inflammation, edema, and nerve root compression, also called, idiopathic polyneuritis or post infectious polyneuritis and Landry's paralysis.

> Also, the classic cerebrospinal fluid findings are of an elevated protein level without an increase in the number of leukocytes. The cerebrospinal fluid pressure is within normal limits.

> The patient care section of this book told me that:

> There is no special treatment for this disease. It must run its course and for this reason skilled patient care is imperative, particularly in the acute phase when respiratory failure requiring prolonged mechanical ventilation is a very real possibility.

This evidence certainly implied that Phil really could have had Guillain Barré Syndrome soon after he had the flu vaccines. Also, the previous paragraph was indicated in the reports from Dr. Worthy in L.A. regarding the elevated protein level in the spinal fluid. This was also confirmed by Dr. Cooke, in Spokane (1986).

Just prior to Phil's brain biopsy, Dr. Cooke sent one of his reports to Dr. Mackay in which he wrote the following:

> In reviewing my records, Mr. Richardson also has a high spinal fluid protein, 108 mg percent with a high gamma globulin fraction without oligoclonal banding. Perhaps he does have a fungal or tuberculous lesion on the brain, which has produced his communicating hydrocephalus.

> Since the situation is deteriorating clinically, and his wife is pleading for anything that can be done, perhaps we should consider a left frontal lobe biopsy to see if he does indeed have an infectious disease.

Except for a couple of times when Phil was not able to walk for almost a week because of his bad feet, he did not have any visible paralysis. It was his brain which suffered the most damage, almost like certain parts were paralyzed. It is beyond me that he was even able to communicate at all, especially toward the end.

Since the doctor in Irvine had found the slow growing infection on Phil's brain during the P.E.T. scan and said it could in some way be connected to the Swine Flu vaccine, there seemed enough evidence right there. All these incidents seemed to be falling into place like a jigsaw puzzle.

In spite of everything, my efforts to help Phil had all been in vain, but I don't regret any of it. How could I stand by idly and not make the effort when he had such a strong will to live. When I think of all the medical experts involved in the Swine Flu program, and how they were taken off guard when Guillain Barré Syndrome appeared on the scene, it makes me sick. If they didn't know this would happen, how on earth were we supposed to know? Because of this fact, I think both the government and the manufacturers of the flu vaccines were negligent in not putting out more information on the consent forms.

I also think they should have been responsible for Phil's comfort and well being. I realize he did get a disability pension, but he was entitled to that regardless, because of having baker's lung. I just wish he could have stayed home in familiar surroundings and been provided with professional care. Instead he went through all those years of suffering in silent humiliation.

When I told my daughters I was thinking of writing about Phil, they suggested I inquire at one of the local colleges to see if any students of journalism would be able to assist me. No one seemed interested until I spoke with my friend Cindy Miller at EWU library. Cindy advised me to speak to a gentleman named Bill Stimson, an Associate Professor of Journalism at E.W.U. I told Mr. Stimson that my sole purpose in writing was to try to raise money so that I could bring Phil home and help to pay for his care. Most of all, I wanted to take him off the Medicaid Plan because he would be appalled if he knew the situation and this could be my way of working for him.

Mr. Stimson asked me to tell him a little bit about my story and when I was through he just said, "You don't need any help from anyone." He then said, "It is not easy to get a book published, but it's not impossible either, only don't count on it." He said, "Go ahead and write the story regardless because it needs to be told and don't let anyone change it, just write it from your heart and in your own words."

Mr. Stimson made a very good impression on me that day, so much so that I had a feeling of confidence in myself. As I walked out of his office, I felt like one of his students who had just received a good grade. I went home that very day and started to write.

The Vicious Circle Ends

My desire to take Phil home was definitely no reflection on St. Luke's Extended Care Center. In my estimation, this was the best such facility in Spokane. It was just the thought of him being all alone at night. I would lay awake wondering what his thoughts were and wished I could be there to comfort him. The night must have been so lonely.

Phil had a close brush with death in 1991. He developed a serious bladder infection accompanied with high fever and dehydration. This happened while I was gone for a few days vacation with Cathy and Jeff. It was the first time I had been away from him for any extended period of time. However, Heather was now working at St. Luke's as a part-time ward secretary and encouraged me to go because she could visit with him.

They didn't think he would make it until I got home. Once again, he pulled through thanks to the good care and help from his doctor, and I was so thankful Heather was with him.

After this scare, I decided it was time to face reality and I asked Heather when she had time if she would take me to pick out a casket for him. I knew if the time came suddenly it would be too hard on me. Heather arranged a day.

I have to say here that I would fail in my tribute to Phil if I didn't tell about this incident. Heather and I were both trying to say something to lighten the atmosphere as we looked over the various caskets but my only thought was of Phil's sense of humour. I thought back to the bakery where it seemed his humour was at its best. We had a daily routine of keeping a number of decorated cakes in the showcase for customers who forgot a birthday or anniversary and would need one immediately. Phil would just have to write the appropriate inscription on the cake.

There were so many times when people would phone at the last minute just as Phil almost made it out the door. I would then run to catch him and say, "Just a minute Phil, I need you to write on this cake."

One day, on such an occasion, he said to me, "I swear to God, Jess, that when I'm in my casket and they are just about to close it, you will run down the aisle of the church with a cake in your hand and say, 'Just a minute, Phil. I need you to write on this cake.'"

It was about a year later when Phil was thought to have a touch of flu. He was vomiting but the emesis was of a bright orange color and his skin was turning yellow. He was taken to emergency at the hospital where they found he was severely impacted from a bowel obstruction. This was taken care of and he was brought back to his room. At this time, Phil was moved closer to the nurse's station. His new room-mate was Art McCabe, a very good looking man in his late sixties.

Sometime later Phil experienced another bout of vomiting. He was passing blood and there was blood in the vomit which was orange in color, as before. He was taken for x-rays and the results showed another bowel obstruction. When his doctor learned of this she asked to see me.

Heather and I went to see Dr. Finlay in her office which was just across the street from St. Luke's. We were told that, although Phil seemed to pull through these spells, we must assume if they occurred again that he may have cancer of the colon. We asked if surgery could be done and the doctor said yes, but she would not advise it. She didn't think any surgeon would want to operate on Phil in his condition.

I reminded this doctor that she was the one who helped to pull him through his serious illness the year before. She told me, in no uncertain terms, that I couldn't expect to hang on to him forever, but it was difficult to accept that Phil may have or had cancer.

With all due respect to Dr. Finlay, I couldn't understand why Phil was still eager for his meals. One would think if he was that sick, food would be the last thing he wanted after vomiting.

Apart from his skin still a little yellow, he didn't appear in distress. In fact, every afternoon before he was put down for a nap, we had a little ritual. I would stand close to him by the side of the wheel chair then I brought his arms up and put them around my waist. Then came a real "bedroom kiss" (a term one of the aides used when she walked in on us one day). I always told Phil I could feel that kiss all the way down to my toes. His face would light up as he nodded his head as if to say, "Me too." I can still feel the warmth of that embrace.

However, Phil was making more trips to the emergency. One time he was anemic and needed two units of blood. Another time he had pneumonia and a high fever. I was beginning to get very worried. I asked Dr. Finlay if she would mind if I called in a gastroenterologist to examine Phil and she said that was fine with her.

It was a holiday week-end so instead of phoning, I went over to the Deaconess Medical Center and pleaded for someone to come over to see Phil as soon as possible. Early the next morning a specialist, Dr. Frost, was there. After examining Phil and looking over his charts, he took Heather and me out of the room and gave us the diagnosis.

He said that in his opinion, because of the surgery for a shunt which Phil had for treatment of hydrocephalus, it was possible an adhesion had formed from the scar tissue at the site. In turn, this caused a kink in the intestine, consequently, that's where the obstruction was.

Dr. Frost said, "Phil may have a small growth but he doesn't appear to have any pain or discomfort." His diagnosis made more sense to us than the possibility of cancer.

The sad news was that Phil could have surgery done, but he could wind up with a colostomy or a permanent tube feeder.

Either one of these were not advisable in Phil's condition because they could eventually cause severe infection.

Finally, we were told the kindest thing we could do at this point was to let him starve to death. He would be given liquids intravenously to avoid dehydration.

Heather asked the dreaded question for me, "How long will this take."

The doctor replied, "Two weeks."

I felt as though it was I who had just been handed the death sentence. After I got home that night I felt so empty inside. My head was spinning. I couldn't believe this was really happening. Would I make the right decision? "Dear God, help me," I thought to myself.

It was just beginning to sink in that I wouldn't ever be able to bring Phil home again. The very thought was making me hurt all over. I couldn't go to bed. I knew I wouldn't sleep so I got the medical books out. I thought I might find some answers to this final blow. I looked up information on the "shunt" and one excerpt read:

> A disadvantage of the shunt is dilution of the blood and a resultant drop in hematocrit which necessitates transfusion of packed cells and perhaps a slowing of the rate of flow of ascitic fluid in the venous system. Other inherent risks are infection, leakage of ascitic fluid from the operative site, elevated bilirubin, gastrointestinal bleeding, and disseminated intravascular coagulation.

I also learned that bilirubin is an orange bile pigment. Failure of the liver cells to excrete bile or obstruction of the bile ducts can cause an increased amount of bilirubin in the body fluids and this leads to obstructive jaundice.

This information made it clear to me that the opinion of Dr. Frost was correct but more to the point, this was the last piece of the puzzle to complete the vicious circle. If Phil had not been injected with the flu vaccines, he would not have developed hydrocephalus for which he was given a shunt as treatment. If he had not had the shunt, there would have been no adhesion which in turn caused a kink. Then the kink caused the obstruction in the bowel. Now, because it was not advisable for Phil to have surgery (in other words, again he didn't have a chance), I must agree to let him go. The vaccines had won and the vicious circle was finally broken, and so was my heart.

Heather and I decided to do the kindest thing, as Dr. Frost advised us. So now I wanted and needed to spend whatever time Phil had left as close to him as possible. We immediately asked all the family to come and see him before he became too ill to recognize them. After that, we went to the funeral home to make as many arrangements as possible up to that point.

Phil had now been moved upstairs to the medical floor and an NG tube inserted in his nose and through to his stomach. A suctioning device attached to the tube would bring up the contents of his stomach to avoid any infection. After a few days Dr. Finlay ordered some liquids by mouth for Phil. She said it would give him a little nourishment. Consequently, this prolonged the inevitable.

I agreed with Heather that she was sure Phil was aware of what was happening so he would know what our feelings were too. I don't know which is worse, the shock of someone dying suddenly or knowing how long they have left and dreading each day that comes?

Phil had a few days of discomfort when the suction device didn't work properly. He was able to convey this to me by moaning. At these times I would massage his stomach and his legs which by now were just skin and bone. Because he seemed a little sad, I tried to cheer him up by playing tapes of his favourite songs. One day I played bag pipe music. I used my umbrella as a baton and proceeded to march back and forth in his room to the tune of Scotland the Brave. He was propped up in bed and this brought a chuckle from him as he nodded his head to let me know he was enjoying watching me make a fool of myself. I could see his fingers moving to the beat.

As I sat by his bedside each day, I talked about happy occasions like our grand-daughter Cristina and her husband Brain expecting their first child. This would be Heather and Ernesto's first grand-child and our first great grand-child.

I told Phil about Cathy and Jeff taking up ballroom dancing and how well they were doing. I knew he would like that idea. He always thought it was so romantic dancing to beautiful music.

I also reminded him of the many funny things that happened in the bakery, especially on Sunday mornings when the church crowds came in. I asked him how many times he heard the remark, "The cake sure looks awful pretty, Phil."

To which he always replied, "How can it be pretty if it looks awful." He would say to me later, "I thought we were the only ones with the strange vocabulary."

Now that he was about to leave this world, what else could I talk about other than whatever made him happy. His work in the baking industry was the biggest part of his life.

I suddenly remembered something that made me sad, the time when I lost my precious wedding ring. It was the day we went to apply for Social Security benefits. There was snow on the ground, and when I got out of the car, I put my hand in the top of my slacks to push my sweater down. In doing this, and because my hands were very cold, I must have pushed down so hard that both my rings came off and down my slacks onto the ground.

I didn't realize this until we were in the S.S. office and looked at my hands. I immediately panicked and started to cry. We went outside and looked all over but didn't find them. The snow made it difficult so we left our phone number with a young black man who was in charge of the parking lot.

Later that afternoon the attendant called to tell us he had found the engagement ring but not the wedding ring. I was so happy, at least to get my special little ring back, and I offered the young man some money, but he wouldn't take it. He said the smile on my face was enough reward for him. I put a notice in the paper offering a reward for my wedding ring, the one with Phil's scroll engraved on it, but it was never found. My good friend Mrs. Lunz gave me a nice, gold band to replace it.

It was now the first of July and Phil was alert enough to greet the many friends who dropped in to see him, if only with a nod of his head. Most of the aides came by during their break and Ethelee McCabe (Art's wife) brought Art up in his wheel chair to visit for a while.

I am reminded of a pleasant experience I had which I knew Phil wouldn't mind me telling him again. He was already in the nursing home in April of 1990, and the famous singer, Engelbert Humperdinck was appearing at the Spokane Opera House. He had been there before, but we were out of town and Phil always said for me not to worry, we would see him if he comes here again.

This happened to be the anniversary of our first meeting fifty-seven years ago at a dance in the Bently Pavilion. I knew that Phil would want me to see this man, not only because he was a great singer, but he is also one of our countrymen and had lived not far from my home town. I was lucky enough to get a ticket at the last minute and the opera house was packed. I could not keep still in my seat and swayed from side to side in tune with every song. I was reliving that first night at the dance all over again. When it came to one of our favourites, "The Last Waltz", tears were streaming down my face as I thought of how we danced the last waltz together and how I wished that night would never end.

As I was leaving, I saw a small crowd making their way to the back stage door and I said to myself, "Why not?" I wanted to get a closer look at this handsome singer of beautiful songs. I joined the crowd outside, which began to dwindle as it got quite chilly. After a period of waiting, I mentioned I would have to be leaving to catch the last bus. A lady who was there with her two daughters spoke up and asked where I lived. She then told me they would be going right by my street on their way home, 80 miles north of Spokane to Colville, and would be happy to give me a ride.

The stage door finally opened and the singer came down the steps to sign autographs. I caught sight of a very tall man and asked him to take a picture of Engelbert for me with my camera.

To my surprise, this young man called out, "Hey, Bert. How about a picture here with this little lady," as he pushed his way through.

The next thing I knew, Bert was bending down with his cheek close to mine and he said, "You know you're just adorable."

I didn't swoon like some younger person might have done. I just thought of Phil's humour and the times when he used to thank the nurses for taking care of him. This one particular time he said to one nurse, "Your generosity is only exceeded by your personal beauty."

The nurse replied, as she professed to swoon, "Oh, I feel like a queen." Then she added, "I know you are just trying to make me feel good."

That's how I felt about the great Engelbert Humperdinck. He was just trying to make me feel good, and he certainly succeeded. I couldn't wait to see Phil's face when I told him.

I tried to remember many stories like this one to tell Phil. I also took pictures for him to look at, hoping he could see them well enough. These were of the most unusual cakes he made, like the replica of Spokane's International Airport Terminal for their fifth anniversary. They were having a big celebration. I reminded him of the few nights sleep he lost, not over making the cake, he always enjoyed that kind of challenge, but how he was going to get it to the airport in one piece. This turned out to be another real masterpiece and was a huge success. It also got coverage on local television.

One day I took a plaque that he earned after taking flying lessons. He successfully completed his first solo flight in a Piper Cherokee in 1965. I wanted him to see it one more time because he was so proud of it. Phil gave credit for this achievement to flight instructor, Charles Delp at Felts Field in Spokane, Washington.

It was now July 5th, and we had just had three or four days of relentless rain and bad thunderstorms. It was such dark, grey weather. While Phil slept, I spent time looking out of the window. My thoughts were sometimes miles away. Often when I would turn around, his eyes would search for me with a look of concern that seemed to say, "Have you got a problem, Jess?"

I would get close to him and say, "Don't worry, I am OK."

He would then nod his head and go back to sleep.

Sometime ago I had crocheted an afghan for his bed and now that he was sleeping a lot he would snuggle down with it. This reminded me of a child with a security blanket.

He was getting weaker and looked very tired. I felt so very sad inside, but I had to try and keep his spirits up. I finally told him I was writing about our lives together and about all the good times we had experienced. This brought forth a raised eyebrow and quite a few nods of his head which told me he approved.

It was easy to talk about the grandchildren because I knew he felt proud of them. He was especially proud of how Sandro and Cristina had excelled in art work. I told him that they must have inherited some of his artistic talent.

Sandro now had a good job in graphic arts. He was head of the art department with a printing firm in Seattle where he lived with his wife, Susan. Cristina was living in Bellingham with her husband Brian Drew. She was hoping someday to have her own art studio.

Simonetta was also living in Bellingham. I would describe her as an extremely happy and caring person. She had an infectious laugh and loved to go hiking with her friends.

Cathy's oldest boy, Chad, was becoming a whiz with computers.

Luke, I'm sure could charm anyone with his rendition of classical music on the piano. I think there was also a good chance he could follow in his dad's footsteps to the basketball courts.

What I wouldn't give if Phil could only see all of these things. He was now taking very little liquids and by Friday, July 10th, he was refusing anything. The next day his breathing became very labored so he was given oxygen. The mask irritated him and he tried to press his face into the pillow to get rid of the tube.

Finally, I said what I knew he would say, if he could only speak, "These bloody tubes!" That brought a chuckle from him and a nod of his head.

I went home that day with Heather at 4:30 p.m. Phil seemed quite comfortable but around 7:00 p.m. the nurse phoned to say she thought he was failing. We dropped everything and after a fast call to Cathy, we went back to St. Luke's. The nurse was apologizing thinking she acted too hastily, but I told her not to worry. I was happy she wasn't taking any chances.

Heather left at midnight, she had to be back on duty by 7:00 a.m. the next morning. When I thought it was safe, I climbed on top of Phil's bed so that I could lie close to him and he could feel I was there. I would have gotten under the covers with him but it was almost impossible because of all the tubes attached to him.

During the night when the nurse came in to check his vital signs, I pretended to be sleeping in case she might tell me to move. The creaking noise of the velcro on the blood pressure cuff sounded so loud in the stillness of the night and so did every breath that Phil took.

The next morning (Sunday, July 12th) I got down from the bed just before Heather came in the room with a male nurse. He wanted to take Phil's vital signs before going off shift. He told me Phil's heart was still strong but the rest of him was failing.

As soon as the day nurse, Terri, and the aide, Sharon, arrived, I phoned my good neighbor, Mr. Cox to come and get me. I needed to go home for a quick shower and a change of clothes. I wanted to be prepared in case Phil went into a coma. The nursing home would provide a cot so that I could sleep in the room.

Mr. Cox came for me right away and had me back again in no time. He was surprised to see Phil was awake but looking very tired. I settled down in his wheel chair by the side of the bed and watched him fall asleep.

At 11:00 a.m., Sharon came in to turn Phil over again. I talked to him for a while and pulled his afghan closer around him. It was a hot day but the air conditioner was on which made it chilly. He snuggled down in his favourite spot on his side with his legs in a fetal position and again I watched him fall asleep, still clutching to the afghan.

At 11:30, Heather came in his room. This was her lunch break. She told me to go to the cafeteria and get some lunch while she kept watch. I was gone about twenty minutes and when I got back Heather went to her station which was close by.

I just got settled down again when suddenly Phil's heavy breathing stopped. I called out for Terri and she in turn called Heather to come quick. As I got closer to Phil, I saw him give a deep sigh like it came from the soles of his feet. Terri put her stethoscope to his chest and said he was still with us but just barely. Heather was at the other side of the bed, and we saw him take a short breath and flap his lips and that was it, he was gone in his sleep.

Heather gave a soft cry of sorrow while my tears just flowed as we watched Terri check his eyes then close them. I couldn't believe he had gone so suddenly. They left me alone with him for a while, and I held him close and spoke to him softly.

I felt terrible, yet, I knew he was no longer in any distress. The love of my life was gone just like the flicker of light from a candle. It was that simple. It was so peaceful, for which I will always be thankful. He had already suffered enough.

I waited for Heather to say her good-bye to Phil and then she took me home. The next morning we went to the funeral home to complete all the arrangements and were told we could see Phil that evening.

I couldn't wait to see him. I wanted to rid myself of the sight of him entangled in all those tubes. I was so happy when I saw how nice he looked. He always had such clean looking skin with no blotches or wrinkles. He looked just like the distinguished English gentleman that he was.

Now I could let him go. "Good night my love, I love you."

I remember the day I met you,
the day God made you mine.
I remember the day God took you,
I will to the end of time.

Author Unknown

THINGS I'LL REMEMBER BEST

For many years it's illness that has been Phil's test;
now that he is at peace, it's these things I'll remember best.

Phil's cakes with decorating done so neat;
delicate roses and draped icing, to the eyes a treat.

Phil's cup of tea, close at hand and fixed just right;
prepared by Jess every morning, noon and night.

His cars, for him things of joy and pride;
most important, always a smooth ride.

The Olds, the Chrysler, a shiny blue hearse he would ride;
delivering cakes to the east, west, north and south side.

Phil worked long hours often stressed to the brink;
but seldom missed the chance for a joke and a wink.

A master baker, the likes of I've never seen;
Phil could make things come to life on his white icing screens.

Aside from baking, an avid fisherman was Phil;
what fish he could catch with his rod and his reel.

A mountain lake called Trapper was a story he often told;
Phil shared it with such passion that the story never grew old.

His prize fish mounted on a plaque on the wall;
our trips to Badger Lake before school in the fall.

With a limit of twelve, Phil would fish like mad;
and somehow, when he got home it was thirteen that he had.

Before leaving the lake, on the water Phil would spit;
carefully marking the lake where the next time we'd sit.

For Phil, picking blackberries was always a treat;
to be buried in vines from his head to his feet.

From the bushes you would only hear thrashing about;
then breaking the silence you would hear Phil shout.

Just look at the size of these, look at that one;
for Phil, a bowl of the biggest was a job well done.

Even in sickness, Phil did not change a bit;
he found ways to communicate his good nature and wit.

From a wiggling foot to an eyebrow raised high;
or puckered up lips to kiss Jess on the sly.

Now that the years of illness can be put to rest;
it's these things of Phil I'll remember best.

Jeff McAlister,
Son-in-law

Epilogue

After Phil was laid to rest, I was encouraged to take a vacation and to continue my story. I decided to go to England and spend some time with my family and our good friends, the Stenton's. I also went to visit Phil's sister Edith.

I spent a week in Scotland with the Stenton's. They took another friend along, Edith Pepper, with whom I shared a room. This was a real treat. I had never been to Scotland before. Even though it rained almost every day, we didn't let it dampen our spirits.

We travelled as many of the high roads and low roads as we could reach during the time we had. This was such beautiful country. We saw many lochs and waterfalls and toured many ancient castles. I think the real highlight for me was a, never to be forgotten, boat ride on the famous Loch Lomond. My only regret was that Phil was not able to share this incredible experience with me.

After resting a few days, we then toured more of Yorkshire and we had a guided tour of the magnificent Castle Howard. All of this brought back wonderful memories of Phil and me together. These friends really knew how to provide me an escape from my sadness.

I now just have one sister left in England and several nieces and nephews. My oldest sister, Lucie, died a few years ago.

Those whom I visited with were well aware of Phil's humor, especially his sister.

Many times in the past I was asked, "How do you live with this clown?"

I always replied, "I don't know how I could live without him."

I have to live without him now, but he will always be in my heart and I only have to think of his humor to bring a smile to my face.

I wish I could have told him that, when I was in Scotland, I finally uncovered the mystery of what the Scotsmen wear under their kilts. That would have made him laugh.

As I said good-bye to our long-time friends, Dot and Joe Stenton, and their family; little did any of us know those happy times would be my last ones with dear Dorothy. She passed away just recently, quite unexpectedly. If I ever take another trip to England, somehow Yorkshire just won't be the same.

Later in the year 1992, around Christmas time, I was going through papers and pictures, and I came across a Christmas card that Phil had given me. It was at least ten years old and must have been the last time he was able to write. He had written a few lines on the inside and started by wishing me a Merry Christmas, Happy Birthday and Happy Anniversary, saying they were all long overdue and to forgive him for all the mistakes. Among other terms of endearment, he also wrote, "Maybe what we both need is a trip to Doncaster, eh? And to see Libby." He ended with, "I send you all my love, Phil." On the bottom of the card was his usual trademark scroll which was around my wedding ring.

These few lines projected something very special to me. It was not only what Phil wrote but the writing itself. There was only one mistake. My mother had already passed away but her name was Libby and Doncaster was my home town where we first met. The scroll was a little shaky, being out of practice, but nevertheless; it was there. Was this the work of a person with Alzheimer's disease? I think not!

It wasn't too long after he had written the card that the Aphasia must have struck him, and unfortunately, we weren't aware of it for so long.

I remember trying so hard, day after day, to encourage him to write because he used to do such a good job. I couldn't even get him to write his name.

Whenever he was being evaluated, there were so many times he was not able to respond. According to medical information, that could possibly be because Aphasics often have difficulty reacting to the normal pace of speaking. They were not able to handle too many words and messages at one time.

Although finding that card, after Phil's death, was very emotional for me; I told myself that I was not going to be sad over it. As a matter of fact, it was just what I needed to get me through this first Christmas without him. How could I not bring myself to be happy at this time, his most favourite time of all?

Just a few weeks later, our first great grandchild was born. I think my first glimpse of this beautiful little girl, Sara Jessie, helped a lot to ease my pain.

* * * * * * * * * * *

I would like to thank the many people, outside of my own family, who helped me through all the years of frustration. First on the list is all the doctors and nursing staff at St. Luke's Memorial Hospital where Phil was provided with such tender loving care. They were just wonderful, especially those in the intensive care unit. I can't speak too highly of them. I regret that this hospital is no longer in existence. I know that I speak for many people when I say that this small, but warm and friendly hospital will be sadly missed. It was because of my faith in the hospital that I chose their nursing home for Phil when the time came. I have never regretted it and will continue to sing their praises.

I must also express my appreciation to all those who helped me to get through the almost three years at St. Luke's Extended Care Center. This includes everyone from the administration to the nurses, the CNA's and housekeepers. They always treated me with the utmost respect. We all had a lot of fun at times, especially with some of the aides who were there from the beginning to take care of Phil, like Kathy

Aldrich and Michelle Porter. I'm sure, if Phil could have spoken, he would have showered Michelle with his humor. Like me, he would have seen the beauty within her. Michelle's face exuded sunshine and joy to all the residents who loved her. I'm sure I gave her many headaches in my attempt to pick her brains.

Special thanks to my two volunteer friends at St. Luke's, Colleen Pounder and Jerry Scollard. They gave so much of themselves over the years with their caring and countless hours of entertaining the residents. They surely brightened many a day for the residents which might otherwise have been a lonely existence. The two of them sort of adopted me along the way and, on occasion, would sit with Phil to give me a break. They also added their names to my long list of private chauffeurs.

To each and every one, my sincere thanks.

In conclusion, I would like to pay a tribute to a lady with a big heart. This lady has been stricken with a terrible affliction. She is now almost blind because of diabetes. I am in awe of her tenacious courage, in spite of her handicap. She still manages to volunteer at the Spokane Civic Theatre. She has been associated with this theatre for more than twenty-five years. She always introduced me as her friend from James Herriot's, "Yorkshire." This always gave me such a lift. I was sure I would eventually grow but no such luck.

So to you, Beverly Lundquist,
thank you for constantly reminding
me to hang in there.

May God bless you and light the
way through your path of darkness.

Sincerely,

Jessica Richardson,
Your Best Friend